FRANC AMOUR

FRANC AMOUR

Lesley Goldie

Paperback ISBN: 9798300412425

Cover painting © Mungo Powey
Book and cover design by Bridget Morley

Text copyright ©2024
Lesley Goldie has asserted her right under the Copyright Design
and Patents Act 1988 to be identified as the author of this work.
All rights reserved. No part of this publication may be reproduced,
stored in or introduced on to a retrieval system or transmitted, in
any form, or by any means (electronic, mechanical, photocopying
or otherwise) without written permission of the author. Any person
who does any unauthorised act in relation to this publication may
be liable to criminal prosecution and civil claim for damages.
This book is sold subject to the conditions that it shall not, by way
of trade or otherwise, be lent, resold, hired out or otherwise circu-
lated without the author's prior consent in any form of binding
or cover other than that in which it is printed.

For Douggie and Ciaran

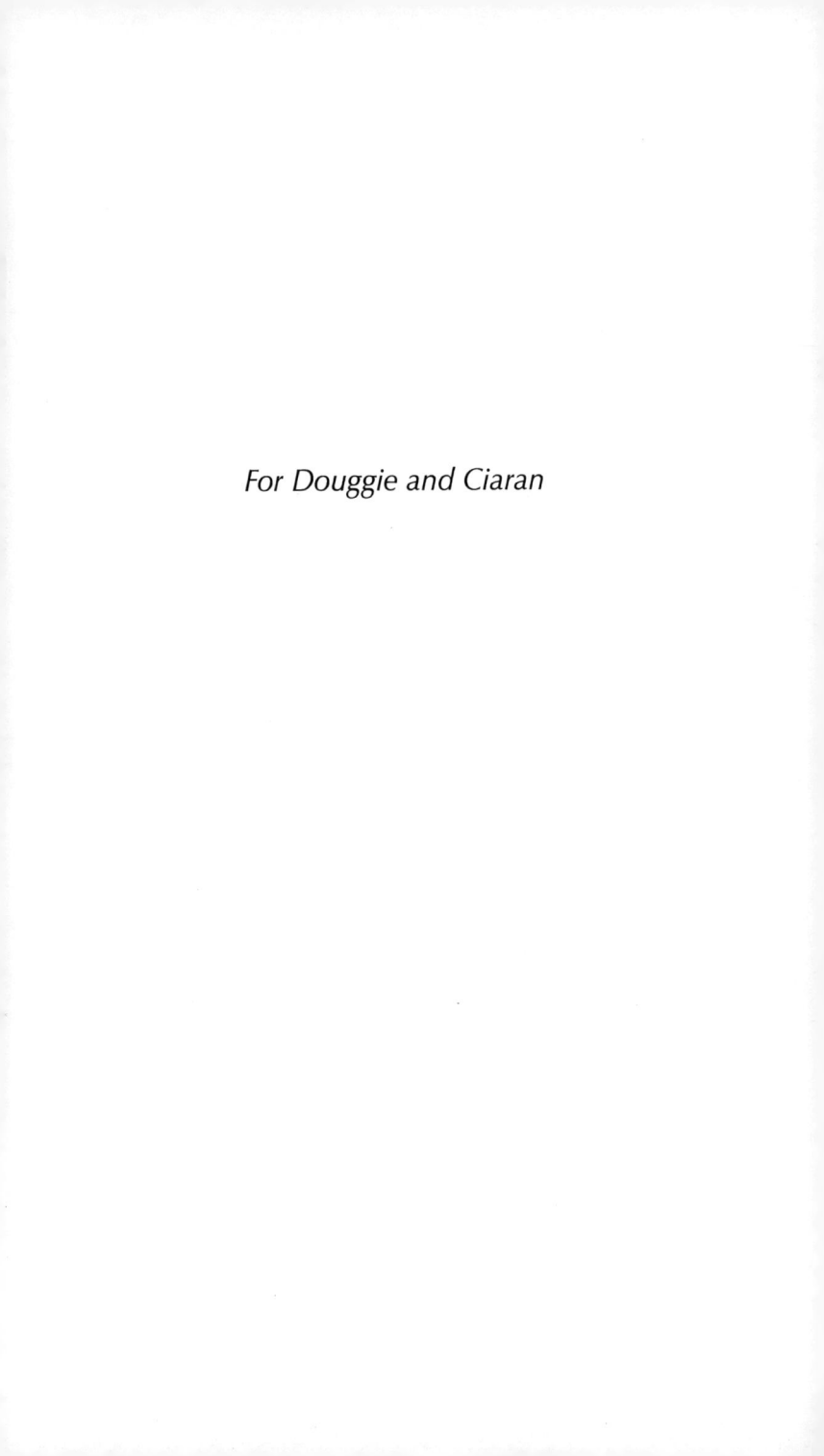

CONTENTS

CHAPTER 1	That was a bloody awful start!	1
CHAPTER 2	Get thee to a nunnery!	6
CHAPTER 3	One night only in Provence	10
CHAPTER 4	The streets were paved with gold	14
CHAPTER 5	Of pills and pillows	19
CHAPTER 6	The long and winding road to *le prieuré*	24
CHAPTER 7	Just a little detour picking up a most unwelcome friend	28
CHAPTER 8	Chez nous *le prieuré*	35
CHAPTER 9	And those that came with it	38
CHAPTER 10	The annual ritual	45
CHAPTER 11	Going back to the jippy tum	52
CHAPTER 12	The wildlife within	55
CHAPTER 13	And there was more …	58
CHAPTER 14	Seventeen years and the big rift	63
CHAPTER 15	Transitioning	69
CHAPTER 16	Never mind the Bayeux … the tapestry that was La Garde Freinet	72
CHAPTER 17	*La canicule* 2003	76
CHAPTER 18	Love France, pity about the French!	82
CHAPTER 19	Thank you Benny	87
CHAPTER 20	And that's life	93
CHAPTER 21	Messing about on the water	98
CHAPTER 22	On fine dining or otherwise	102
	Epilogue	108

CHAPTER 1

That was a bloody awful start!

Love affairs start in many strange ways, but mine with France got off on the wrong foot – big time.

Our French Trinitarian Convent in Bromley, Kent hosted suitable girls for exchange, and I can't remember exactly, but I guess that's how I got hooked up to go and stay with a French girl, Caroline.

It wasn't my first visit to France, but previously it had only been en passant on the way to Switzerland (considered more civilised), sitting in the back of our family's little black Austin 8, always stocked up with homemade sausagemeat pies. I think my mother was under the impression that we were unlikely to find anything fit to eat once we had crossed the Channel. These certainly were not, by the time I had sat on them for two days, invariably calling out to stop the car so I could be sick. I was a dreadful traveller back then. Never mind, we sported a proud, jaunty Union Jack flag fluttering on the bonnet and waved manically if we passed another British car. A rare occurrence in the years just after the end of the Second World War.

This was France after what novelist Irène Némirovsky called 'her darkest hour' – primitive houses opened directly onto the *routes nationales*, women, often barefoot, could be seen lugging bales of straw upon their backs. This was France decimated by two

World Wars, before the Marshall Plan, signed in 1948, lifted it from its rubble and began the process of crisscrossing it with magnificent autoroutes and restoring civilisation to this beautiful country that had so suffered.

However (having digressed, which I warn you, I do a lot), back to Caroline. At the age of twelve, this was to be my first stay on my own in France with another family. Having never been anywhere apart from a few sleepovers at friends' houses, it was for me a huge and rather terrifying yet exciting leap into the unknown for a very sheltered and quite timid young suburban girl. I was to be driven to Newhaven by my parents and put on the ferry, where I would be met in Dieppe by my host's family. One can only imagine the abuse Kirstie Allsopp would have endured, had there been social media!

Geared up, nervous, excited the night before the journey, I looked in horror to see blood in the loo. My period had finally started. What a measure of how life has changed since the 1950s! I knew nothing about it, was totally not prepared. My mother, who, sexually buttoned up, believed that sex was only to have babies, had not even discussed it with me nor prepared me on how to cope. Fortunately, my rather more forthright aunt was staying and took the matter firmly in hand, giving me the lowdown on the practicalities.

So, off I went to stay first in a beautiful apartment in the Place de la Madeleine with a very elegant, sophisticated family where we breakfasted on tartines and croissants with coffee – real coffee, not Camp Coffee – served in bowls, not cups and saucers. The poor, lovely Maman must have wondered whatever the Brits had washed up on her shores, as she dutifully and very kindly guided her two daughters and this snivelling, miserable, lost and bewildered teenager around all the amazing sights of Paris: Notre Dame, the Louvre, the Seine – the Musée D'Orsay was not created then.

She must have wondered why this miserable English kid never seemed to cheer up. Yes, I was homesick, but mostly I was worried sick about who to turn to and how to ask for STs (sanitary towels. These, dear readers, were pre-Tampax days). Where to buy them and, even more embarrassingly, how to dispose of them. Having helped me cope with the first problem, things got a little easier. I felt somewhat more reassured and supported, and she was able to understand me more.

Gradually, I became impressed by the beauty around me and actually enjoyed the excitement of the grand boulevards, the Champs-Élysées and the glitter and sophistication of Galeries Lafayette. I remember, with some pride, buying some take-home gifts – a pair of little white kid ankle boots for my eighteen month-old sister and an amazing bottle opener like a zig-zag, really ahead of its time, for my parents. Which, on reflection puzzles me, as my father virtually never drank, except for the occasional bottle on significant occasions.

What is fixed in my memory is the week we spent (that is, the kids) at the grandparents' home in Épernay, I think it was. A large, rustic farmhouse in a small rural village on the outskirts of Paris – it is probably a *banlieue* (suburb) now. There seemed to be two staff, a cook and a housekeeper, and each day we children took a couple of milk churns up to a farm to be filled for the day. The atmosphere of that place, the way of life, the rural simplicity and the quiet beauty impressed a lasting memory on me, and was, I think, the beginning of my deep love of rural France. The downside was that the toilet was located at the far end of the garden.

We kids – all four or five of us, I think – slept at the top of the house in a converted *grenier* (attic). Imagine, then, the further trauma that beset this English suburban girl, coping with her first period, which lasted ten days. No way could I get through the night, so this meant a torchlight descent down two flights of stairs and a walk to the end of the garden to deal with the complexities of newly acquired 'women's problems.' And then, even more horrors – how to dispose of the bloody hoard I had now accumulated in my suitcase.

Finally, I plucked up the courage to ask the housekeeper in my best French, '*Est-ce que je peux mettre quelque chose dans le feu?*'. Thank goodness she seemed to grasp the need and lifted the lid on the big old boiler in the kitchen, relieving me.

One thing I remember taking away from my time shared with Caroline was learning a little about cooking. She introduced us to crêpe aux champignons.

Make up a usual pancake batter à la Delia, and with a hot pan and unsalted butter, fry your thin crêpes (pancakes). In another pan, put chopped mushrooms and simmer in unsalted butter, salt, pepper and then garlic (herein was the magic ingredient that hit me in the 1950s), and a dash of Lea & Perrins sauce. Spread the mixture on the first crêpe, add a crêpe, and so on like a cake. Sprinkle a little grated cheese to melt on top, then take a slice out and serve with salad dressed with vinaigrette, which I also learnt from her. Et voilà.

CHAPTER 2

Get thee to a nunnery!

It was as if it were all preordained ... the convent school I went to in England was a French Trinitarian order ... I hasten to add, not at all like St Trinian's. It was the Holy Trinity Convent, Bromley. Unlike most of my friends, and those still alive, I loved my school very much. It was a beautiful, large Georgian house set in wonderful grounds, with magnificent ancient cedar trees and an outdoor swimming pool.

My father, an aspirational son of a Welsh mining family, whose father was an alcoholic and never spoken of in our house, had trained and qualified himself at night school as an engineer. He was determined that his daughter should be socially upwardly mobile. Though this was never framed in those terms at that time, she was going to be educated and genteel, and might one day run a tearoom! The height of expectations for a career woman then.

So when the state refused to recognise my 11-plus, allowing me free education in an Roman Catholic school (it being only available to Catholic pupils), he fought hard to beat the system. As the Reverend Mother was all for allowing me there, he won. All credit to him, I don't know how he managed it, but I was the only non-Catholic who passed through those hal-

Some Holy Trinity friends – me 2 from R.

lowed doors on free tuition, free school books, etc. – so I count myself lucky.

However beautiful the environment – and I now realise how fundamentally important that has always been for me – and however lovely the nuns were, the majority of our teaching staff were rubbish ... a bin end load of weirdos, misfits and sadistic saddos apart from my glorious saviour: my English teacher, Miss Hussey, who enthralled me with her love of Shakespeare, Gerard Manley Hopkins, and T.S. Eliot.

But the other glimmer of light, and I must stress that she was a lot larger than a glimmer, was Mademoiselle Duceris, who lived at the convent and taught us kids French. She was, by the standards of those days, hugely fat (today would probably not register very high on the fat Richter scale), greasy, she could never have fitted in a bath and there weren't showers then, and somewhat smelly. We kids, at eleven years old, were absolutely foul to her. We used to put her chair outside the door to air after she left.

And those lessons! A rote learning of the French phonetics '*ou ee ai*', which we had to repeat after her, and which we bastardised into a chorus of gobbledygook. At which she helplessly banged her desk and shouted at us morons, to no avail. And then there was the endless *dictée* – week after week, term after term, year after dreary year. Despite our best efforts to sabotage her teaching, she instilled in us the best French pronunciation and a solid grounding in the language, which I have carried through my life and has given me so much joy.

By the time we reached sixth form, we were all thoroughly ashamed of the appalling way we had treated this poor, kind, unfortunate woman who was quite obviously trapped in the endless cycle of intake of yearly brats, who subjected her to the same. Most of whom ended up feeling remorse and gratitude to her.
I certainly did!

La pauvre mamoiselle

CHAPTER 3

One night only in Provence

About midway through my senior year, another French student, Martine, came to stay. She was very polite, mature and certainly older than I was. I remember her being very well dressed – in that chic way the French have of wearing a twinset and pleated skirt. Funnily enough, one associates twinsets with England, with maiden aunts in the counties and always with pearls.

But at the time, the French couldn't get enough of Marks & Spencer, who were famous for their twinsets. They did set up in Paris, but it didn't work out. Maybe they had gone 'off piste' for a time, because they certainly lost the plot for a few good years until they reinvented themselves, featuring the mature and still gorgeous Twiggy.

The long and the short of it was that Martine passed the test with my appallingly judgmental, narrow-minded and dogmatic parents, and it was agreed that I should go to Aix-en-Provence, her home, and spend three weeks there. My family were off to Alassio – which they moved onto after having done Switzerland – and I was to travel down with them and be dropped off and collected on their return.

It didn't quite work out like that! Aix is a devastatingly beautiful city, with its grand avenues, lined with plane trees, boulevards and fountains shimmering in the blazing heat of the Provence sun and the blinding clarity of the light. The light that drew so many artists to embrace it as the muse for their work: Van Gogh, Cézanne, Picasso, Matisse.

Like most towns and cities in the South of France, the wide streets rapidly give way to very winding, narrow back streets where you can almost shake hands with your neighbour across the street. In Italy, the washing hangs across between the buildings. Bright light gives way to deep shadow, the old stucco buildings – many painted in vivid ochres and pinks, well faded over time – with ironwork railings at opening windows, shutters seemingly shut permanently against the sun, and also against the endlessly rattling mistral. The mistral, the evil wind that rips randomly through regions at speeds of up to 70mph, howling for hours, and mercilessly ripping the pantiles off the shallow roofs, whining through the night at its best for two–three days, and at its worst for up to nine days. It quite literally drives people insane, and the suicide rate soars. The wonderful plus side of this seemingly nightmarish phenomenon is the exquisite clarity of the air, the intensity of the light and the brilliance of the sun – rendering sunglasses an absolute necessity.

Of course, I knew nothing of this as I sat in the back of the car (we had definitely upgraded from an Austin 8 by then) as we trawled through ever-narrowing back streets until eventually we found the house. Well, in our conventional English terms, it didn't really translate. What we arrived at was a huge old stone building with a very large opening. Through the opening was a flight of stone stairs and a metal balustrade. All quite normal in that part of the world, but to us lower middle-class Brits, it was completely alien.

My mother was appalled! This was then heightened by the fact that we had to climb over very large, well-gnawed dog bones littering the stairs, left by the many stray dogs. We finally arrived at what was the second or third floor and knocked on the door. We were warmly welcomed into a sparsely furnished home and introduced to Martine's family. It soon became clear that, to make room for me as a paying guest, their son had to give up his room and stay at the grandparents'.

My parents were totally uneasy and indicated a need to speak privately to me. There was no way they were leaving me there, and I was to come up with an excuse, and they would come by and pick me up in the morning and take me to stay with them in Italy. I was awake most of the night, so distressed at what I had to do. I was compliant and very much used to doing as I was told. But this seemed so rude, so offensive. These people were lovely, very kind, very caring – not a load of roughnecks, or anything like that. They did not deserve to be treated like this, especially as they had gone to so much trouble to accommodate me.

So through the night, I chewed my pen and agonised. Finally, I penned the following note which is indelibly printed on my brain ...

'*À cause des événements imprévus, je suis obligée de retourner chez moi avec mes parents.*'
'Because of unforseen events, I must return home with my parents.'

Leaving this note, I scuttled down the stairs before anyone was about, and to my shame, I left, thereby delaying experiencing the wonders of Aix for many years and retaining a stain on my conscience forever.

CHAPTER 4

The streets were paved with gold

I am talking about the late 1950s to early 1960s when about 5% of girls went to university. In those grand days, we did not go to 'uni'; god how I hate that expression and the degradation it accords it. We went 'up' to university or more often to college. I was determined I would go to Bristol to study drama, as by then, along with my passion for horses and my boyfriend, Michael Johnson (later Michael York), it was my passion. So off I went on the train in a newly bought most horrible voluminous coat with bracelet-length sleeves, all the way to Bristol on my own.

I don't remember much except the actual interview, which was terrifying. I had three heads of dept., English, History and Drama, all grilling me with questions like 'Was King Lear a Christian play?' Fair enough, I should have been able to give a considered response. Perhaps I did.

What I did not do was produce anything substantial in the way of dramatic experience. We did not do school plays, apart from the nativity in which I played the innkeeper in a very common, rough voice, which was considered to be letting the school down! And Pierrot in a local drama group. Somehow I was always cast as the male. It's a good job it was not in today's climate or I might have been having serious thoughts about my gender! Not much else to offer other than the various scenes from Shakespeare I had produced for various festivals – extracts from Macbeth and Richard III very much à l'Olivier – who I adored. Other classmates had pictures of Bill Hayley and the Comets, and Elvis pinned inside their desks. Mine was plastered with those of Olivier in all his many roles, even his cigarette ads, which still remain in my precious inherited book of Shakepeare 1929. It seems I had one literary ancestor!

But, alas, I was not offered a place for drama, English yes, History yes, but Drama NO. It was at that time the only university offering a drama course, in conjunction with the Bristol Old Vic. Devastated, I returned to Bromley, my first real dose of rejection and in a major huff. That was it! I was not going to 'uni'. Well, that was until my beloved English teacher, Miss Hussey, talked some sense into me. 'Come along Lesley, apply to London Queen Mary College', where she had studied, and read English. And I did and I got a place. Completely the wrong choice of course as it turned out, as it was very linguistics oriented, which was not my passion.

However, that was soon more than compensated for by the opportunities it offered with its amazing theatre in the People's Palace, part of the campus in the Mile End Road. I soon came to consider the streets of the Mile End Road not covered with litter, but paved with gold. I loved it there. Big time!

Term had barely started, and I walked into the theatre, where they were auditioning for Bertolt Brecht's *'The Good Woman of Setzuan'*. It was terrifying. The place was full of hippies, beatniks, bearded men, and women with heavy black kohl eye liner, and the swearing! I had never heard a swear word, apart from 'bugger' – which my mother used to say, totally oblivious of its meaning. So in my neat pleated skirt and sweater I rapidly acquired a new four-letter word vocabulary, read for and got the lead part of Shen Teh – the Good Woman.

That was indeed a life-changing moment for me. I morphed from being a reasonably acquiescent, polite schoolgirl, somewhat bullied by one of my classmates for years, which had done little for my self-confidence, to a young person who walked on air, chosen as Miss Fresher, given leads in all the productions for three years, including an offer to play Lady Macbeth for the university, and then elected woman vice president and made an honorary member when I left – with a poor degree – but we'll pass swiftly over that. Was there ever such an opportunity to flourish?

Two summers were spent on the Fringe at the Edinburgh Festival, travelling up in the top of a lorry on top of all the sets and costumes, and living on the fourth floor of a tenement that was due for demolition. We literally had to sweep the rubble off the stairs to get up to the flat, which was completely bare apart from a cooker of sorts, a sink and a loo. No shower or baths.

The guys had to hotfoot it to Loch Lomond to pick up bunk beds from the Sally Army and the rest of us shopped for gas mantles, the only means of lighting. Well it was an experience. We did wash – once a week at the public baths. Rubbish piled up against the kitchen walls until finally someone decided an effort to take it down to the street was necessary

The second year we took Arthur Miller's play *A view from the Bridge*, in which I played Beatrice. It was a nice change from young female leads. We had a brilliant Eddie – a guy with a real chip on his shoulder. If he is still alive he will be a leftish activist. When he was stabbed, he spat his blood capsule straight at the front row of the audience. Not necessarily a very endearing guy but a powerful performer.

We had been invited to take the production to France when we finished at the Fringe, to perform at two venues, Rouen and Rheims. My boyfriend, an engineer from the same college, had a red MG sports car and he decided to come along, so I travelled in somewhat more style. We were hosted by various people who gave us board and lodgings in their homes and didn't seemed concerned that we weren't married. The French were more liberal on the question of l'amour, certainly than we were in England at the time. One quite smart period house where we stayed that had escaped the bombings (there were large spaces between many of them) had a very elegant toilet situated on a dais with steps leading up to it. It struck me as very grand but maybe it was to accommodate the plumbing.

To approach the house we had to park the car and walk across the bombed site of the adjacent house where all the locals and beggars camped out. At first it seemed quite frightening passing by them at night but they were always friendly and not at all threatening. Fortunately.

The theatre we played in was something else, bijou one might say, like a doll's house, with a traditional proscenium arch and seating probably 100. There was one dressing room, shared by male and female alike but the loo situation was more challenging. There wasn't one. We had to go out back into a courtyard, completely black and we very swiftly realised that we shared it not just with blokes but with rats. So we evolved a system of having one guy on guard with a torch to keep the rats away while the girls had a quick pee. The fellas had to fend for themselves.

CHAPTER 5

Of pills and pillows

Many years were to pass with little contact with France except for our memorable visit to Spain, driving through. When college ended, for some bizarre reason I didn't go to graduation, four of us, Doug and I and still our dear friends, Rod and Dot, bought an old, and I mean old, dormobile which we named the 'pig' and set of for Spain with one tent. The journey passed uneventfully enough in that I don't remember anything significant except the general excitement of setting off, with a real sense of adventure. We drove through rural France – I say we, but I didn't drive as I didn't learn until were living in the USA and I was probably twenty-five by then. So the guys drove, and we took turns at sleeping in the tent alternating with nights in the Pig.

The one memory I do have, is of the appalling loos in the campsites at that time. They were legendary and probably the reason that by the time we reached the Spanish border, I was really ill. Raging fever and sore throat. Of course no such thing as medical insurance had been considered in our giddy days even though Rod was at medical school in Edinburgh and became a marvellous doctor.

So we looked for the flashing green light and found

a pharmacy. Although their loos were dreadful there, pharmacies on the other hand were and are brilliant, space-age institutions of excellence and efficiency. They are so professional that there is always a queue of French, waiting their turn. I love the French but god are they hypochondriacs! I soon learned never to ask a French person how they are because they will delight in telling you every detail of their current maladies. '*Oh j'ai mal à la téte*' or '*mal à la gorge*' and that is just for starters.

The pharmacists there seem to have a lot more scope to dispense than those in our shabby little hole in the wall or remote counters in those places called 'chemists' that we seem to see less and less of. Having patiently waited, the customers leave triumphant, like trophy hunters bearing packets and packets of medication. I am sure it is because of them that antibiotics are becoming less effective.

Anyway, having explained my malaise I was presented with a very large 'thing'. How was I to swallow that? Not possible I thought until it was explained by dint of actions that this was a suppository and had to go up my bum! So back to the awful loos where I had my first encounter with sticking something up my backside. It wasn't pleasant. Goodness, it all happens in France. But as one who had frequently suffered from such maladies in younger years, I can honestly say, I have never made such a swift recovery. The next night we were out dancing and then on to Spain.

Briefly, the detour of my tale into Spain is worth the journey. Excitedly, arriving in Barcelona, we thought 'when in Rome etc ...' and bought tickets for a bullfight. Being-twenty-year-old, naive kids, we thought the whole fiesta atmosphere was great. Dorothy and I fished out a couple of rather crumpled dresses and did ourselves up for a night out. Music, laughter, heat, crowds, not to mention alcohol – it was very infectious.

Arriving at the arena, we collected four cushions to make the stone amphitheatre more bearable, but unfortunately none of us heard the announcement, made in several languages, that throwing cushions was a definite no no. The fight with the first bull and the picadors commenced to a great roar in the evening heat. It was intoxicating. However, I soon became very uncomfortable that the horses were going to get gnawed and horses being one of the great passions of my life, that was not going down very well. Probably three of four bulls were seen off and we were finding the whole spectacle increasingly repulsive.

Then came the final bull and he wasn't having any of it. They threw the works at him but he was not going to be felled. Eventually, the matador was hacking at him and the crowd erupted in displeasure – it was utterly disgusting. All around us the crowd started throwing cushions and anything else handy into the arena and that's what we thought you did, so we hurled ours.

The next thing we knew, we were confronted by the Guardia Civile who hauled Doug off, tried to take Rod, who ran off and ended up in the abattoir, and would have taken us girls, but for the intervention of a very elegant, grey-suited gentleman, obviously with influence, who had a word and they let us go. The place was utter chaos. Those being arrested were mostly tourists and like us they found themselves separated. We finally located Doug who had been herded into a compound with various other nationalities.

Some locals took pity on us and told us he would be taken to a local police station – I reckon they were probably in on this racket and did quite well off grateful tips. I think Rod had reunited with us by then and with the help of the locals we followed the police van. They literally hurled the guys into the back, into a hot, airless space and took them off to jail.

We had a system of taking turns to wear the kitty purse from which we eked out our daily allowance. I was wearing it that day and guessed a fine would have to be paid. I tried to make my way to the reception desk in the Guardia and was simply knocked to the ground with the butt of a gun by one of the police.

I mean, things like that didn't happen in England!

It was hugely shocking – so much so that journalists appeared from nowhere, recording the experiences of the crowd of distraught tourists. At the time it was quite a scandal.

The upshot was we finally got Doug released about 2am, the last one, still protesting his rights and wanting the British Consulate. We hurried him into the Pig and got the hell out of Barcelona, driving through the night and have never been back there since. We later learnt that Franco had thirty machine guns trained on the spectators in case of an insurrection. Such was Spain in the 1960s.

CHAPTER 6

The long and winding road to *le prieuré*

Then there followed a long gap with virtually no contact with France. I was preoccupied with being a very bad mother to a very difficult child who screamed all the time. I did not get a night's sleep for six months Finally, after eleven years he was diagnosed with minimal brain damage resulting from a very premature placenta previa birth. I had not coped with the stomach pump that was necessary to get into theatre for an emergency C section – a total nightmare and the poor child had in that delay been starved of oxygen. At the time none of this, was explained to me. So instead of billing and cooing over a sweet newborn, I wondered why on earth people had babies.

Thus my refuge became my love of theatre and the Questors Theatre in Ealing became my go-to home. Having just had a Caesarean (in those days a full up and down job), I found myself learning to roller skate, pushing the pram, in preparation for my next role in Günter Grass's *Onkel Onkel*. People used to stop me with the pram and smile in cooing and then look up at me and ask 'does it always cry?' 'Always!' Not a very good mother, I was consumed with guilt and felt wholly inadequate.

Eleven years went by, taken up largely with comedy and light entertainment, eventually achieving my Equity card – a very slow business then – and I had it just in time to accept a West End part. Then parts in rep, on tour, plays with Susan Hampshire and Judi Dench, directed by Sir John Giegud, and then, surprise, surprise, a divorce. Followed by a move to rural Norfolk, straight off the West End stage to live the 'Good Life' à la Felicity Kendal with cats, dogs, horses, goats and cabbages.

There were no holidays, just endless grinding slog to make this rundown old forge habitable on no money, just slog.

But while in the Old Forge, where my second child was born, an altogether different experience, we took the fancy of an older, well-heeled couple who lived in a beautiful Georgian house just outside the village. Later, much later, it transpired they were estranged from their own children (who isn't?) and they took a shine to us, constantly moving rubble and shovelling shit and they would throw us the odd cabbage *en passant*. We became, I imagine, their surrogate kids.

They had bought a small, modest end of row cottage in Southwest France in a tiny village called Salles la Valette, in the beautiful douce Charente. After the auction, they had learned that with the house came the massive old 14th-century priory in the garden. Not only was it full of the filth of ages, but beautiful old armoires and dressers and French sleigh beds. Having retrieved all the antique furniture, they didn't quite know what to do with the ruined property.

So, we came into their thoughts – young, a bit bonkers and enthusiastic lovers of France, obviously not averse to lugging barrow loads of rubble and cement. They wondered if we would like to visit them in the Charente and see this pile of rubble in their garden. Perhaps we were just mugs! Well, obviously and totally naively, we jumped at the chance. We piled our young son Ciaran (my second, eleven years later after an ectopic and two miscarriages) in the little most beloved Citroën 2CV and beetled off down to la belle Charente.

What a contrast between their very orderly, modest and easily maintainable cottage and the house, a massive three-storey ruined stone building. Dark, full of debris, massive swathes of black cobwebs curtaining the rooms into sections like drapes, full of bats, pine martins and owls, great holes in the massive old floor boards plugged with corn cobs, and a chicken hutch in the bedroom and inviting graffiti on the walls '*Merde a tous qui dort ici*' (shit on all who sleep here). Not much of a welcome. But there were oggi arches on the windows, two magnificent fireplaces, wonderful stone walls to be transformed into *pierre apparente* (exposed stone). All just waiting for some magic fairy or handsome prince to come and reveal their natural beauty, oh, and make them damp proof and wave some oofle dust over all. But it transpired that we were the ones to wave that magic dust. However, just like the fairy story, there was a maze to find a way through.

CHAPTER 7

Just a little detour picking up a most unwelcome friend

While living in the Old Forge, an annoying woman, who shall be nameless, latched onto me big time. She was the wife of someone who employed my husband so I felt somewhat obligated to tolerate her. One morning, it was a Monday, about 9am, she rang me up to ask me what sunscreen I used! She was the kind of person with too much money and time on her hands and not much intelligence to use it. She seemed to spend her time going to yoga classes and lacemaking and was always on the phone telling you how tiring it all was. These calls usually came when you had carted your child back from the day minders, after a day's work, with the shopping to unload and the dogs and cats to feed and also the goats.

So, in response to her query at 9am on that Monday, I think I replied rather tartly, that I had hardly had a holiday in the last twelve years and therefore was really not an authority on the subject. Which may have led to us packing up the 2CV with essentials and beetling off round France. Always remembering to pack a Phillips screwdriver. You can't go anywhere in a 2CV without one. It has the annoying habit of a door dropping off or a panel coming loose. Rather like driving round in a stylish sardine tin. But you know, in the good old days!!! When the amazing network of French autoroutes wasn't an option, to pootle along the RN and the D roads, lined with plane trees dappling everything with sunlight, was one of the greatest joys of my life. Wouldn't dream of driving one on an autoroute nowadays.

Thus we pootled round 2,000 miles of *L'hexagone* (so named as a hexagon neatly contains the shape of France), from the coast and beaches, through forests, happening upon simple *logis* in which to stay, bars to have a coffee, markets to stoke up with goodies, up through the Jura Mountains and down to the Med, and back up through the Loire. Really, there is not much more worth seeing in life that what France has to offer. I remember, years later when I was afforded the luxury of world travel from India to Machu Pichu and travelling first class, sitting on a cruise boat on the Yangtze, smelling the dreadful fumes coming off the water, having been herded on board by little people who were always in your face, thinking 'Get me out of here! Get me back to France.'

So the first leg of our grand tour took us to see friends who lived in the Juras. Lovely people, Phoebe and Gerard, who lived quite high up on a mountain in a property with no fences. What proved difficult was my two-year-old son, Ciaran, who had a fascination for Wellington boots, regardless of the size or compatibility of a pair, donned any he could find and regularly headed off down the mountain.

Ciaran in 'desespoir!'

Phoebe's youngsters just stayed around and she couldn't understand why mine didn't. What could I say? Just had to keep on running to retrieve him.

She wanted to make a little celebration, and her

mum gave her money to buy steak for about fourteen of us, which was duly barbecued, and a very festive time was had by all. Little did we know what lay in wait for our lives following that fun evening.

Next day we set off to drive through the Massif Central on down to the Côte d'Azur. We had retrieved a small one-man tent from them, which had originally belonged to us and we thought most optimistically that we could sort of manage for a day or two roughing it on a campsite. Thus, we pulled into a site, with no other equipment and proceeded to take the front seats out of the 2CV – it was obliging like that and bash the tent pegs into the hard ground with a rock. We looked up to see the immaculate white trainers, socks and tanned legs of a very cool Swiss camper, sporting the whitest shorts, who bemused at our antics, offered us the loan of a mallet. Not an impressive arrival.

And so, all three of us zipped up tight and snug as bugs in a rug, it started. If you have ever had the trots on a French campsite, with the facilities as they were at that time in the early 1980s, you can imagine the nightmare night I had, plus all those unlucky enough to be around me. It proved not to be a simple 24-hour stomach upset. Having outstayed our welcome on the campsite, we packed up the little we had and set off to stay with friends in the Les Cévennes. It was and still is, I believe, a very wild, *sauvage* area in the south where the friends had a property not unlike the priory.

Having spent the day on the beach, pizzas were ordered by the others – I was still pretty wobbly and not

Les Cévennes sauvages

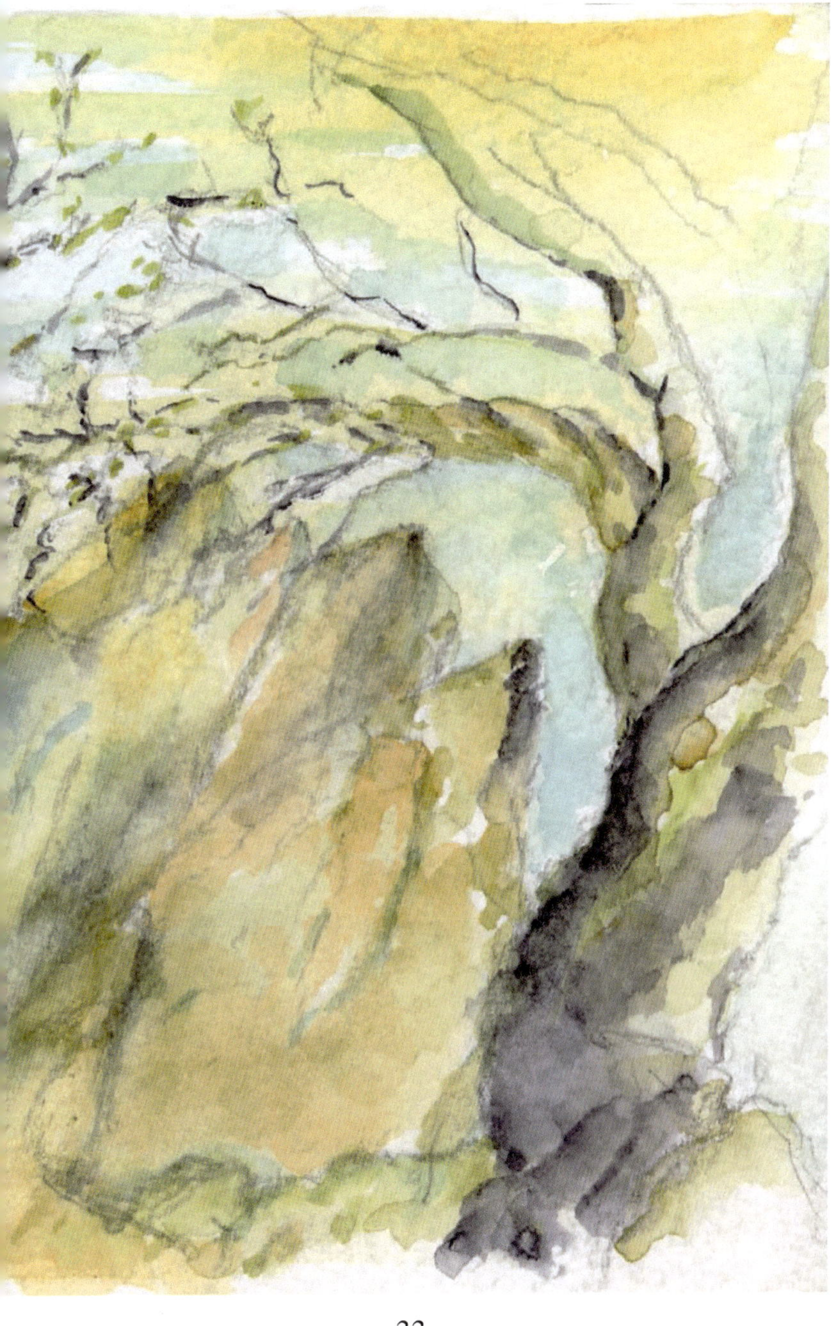

much up for food. My then husband Paul, who was an Irishman who prided himself on his tough physicality, announced we were leaving, and I was to drive as he suddenly felt so ill. Into the 2CV the five of us bundled and I, terrified, had to drive us through the centre of Montpellier in the rush hour. He yelled to pull over, into a supermarket car park where he flung himself out of the car and the unspeakable emerged uncontrollably from both ends of him, at the same time.

Not a scenario I would care to live through again, nor indeed would any of the customers returning to their cars with their trolley loads of groceries. Somehow, all the swimming towels found a new purpose in life, as we endeavoured to curtain him off from view. So with these as a screen and black bin bags, we got him down to the edge of a nearby river (please don't blame me for river pollution!) we cleaned him up as best as possible and back to the house where, after a shower and twelve hours sleep, he emerged recovered and we continued on our travels.

CHAPTER 8

Chez nous le prieuré

During the ensuing two years, we negotiated a very contorted deal, which ended up with us owning the priory. It sounds very grand, doesn't it? Believe me it wasn't. The Rainey's came up with various suggestions as to the deal. Finally they arrived at ours one day and suggested that we should undertake to restore the property to a living standard, they pay for the materials and that at the end of ten years, it should revert to their ownership. I thought I had misheard. Now that was some awkward scenario, but that is what they were suggesting. That we should labour throughout all our summer breaks and at the end of it – what – nothing?. In the friendliest way I knew how, I made it clear that that was not on the table.

So the two men (notice the era!) took a glass of wine out into the garden and came back with the proposition that we give them £4,000 cash and the property would be ours. I have no recall how we raised the cash or how the title deeds were transferred, but that was what we agreed and so we got started.

We spent the next fifteen years, every summer, out there slogging on the project. We had a good arrangement in the end they never used their cottage during school holiday time and as that was the only time we could go, they allowed us to stay rent-free in the cottage next door while we worked. That was great and the deal was that Dorothy always wanted her place spotless – she would exit on sheets of newspaper, like Thora Hird in *Last of the Summer Wine* – so I would always undertake to spring clean their place each year, cupboards, nets, windows and paintwork, and leave it by backing out on sheets of newspaper to finally exit. Truth to tell, I was so intoxicated with life in France that I couldn't wait to use my traditional French broom to sweep all the croissant and baguette crumbs out of the front door, off the pavement and into the gutter, in the style of my local French neighbours. Sad or what?

Ciarán helping with renovation!

So began the long and certainly never finished slog to make the place at least habitable even at a most basic level. Cobwebs swathed like huge black shawls were broomed down, spiders ran, rubbish cleared out, plaster knocked off walls to reveal beautiful stonework needing mortaring and sealing to create *pierre apparante*, ground floor dug out and damp-proof membraned, walls tanked to outside level and cement laid and finally the great achievement, which we paid to be done, of pamments laid throughout the ground floor. They were unsealed so every year I would, on my hands and knees, traffic wax and polish the vast area of them, which is now why I have such knobbly knees. Apart from this, the other major expenditure was the installation of the electrics and the *fosse septique* (septic tank).

CHAPTER 9

And those that came with it

Salles la Valette – such a beautiful name (translates as room of the maid) was a village nestling in the undulating, lush Charente. In the day, there was a boulangerie, a not very smart épicerie and a boucherie run by a feisty handsome woman, not much more. Other than that one relied on the amazing markets that came by local towns certain days of the week, notably Riberac. The pace of life was slow, rhythmic and accompanied through the heat of the summer by the endless humming of the cicadas.

Storms came and went periodically and were often violent and frightening, hence we enjoyed such lush and wooded countryside where sitting outside in the setting evening sun until 10pm at night was such a joy. Or sitting eating simply in one of the many little rustic restaurant under a Paulownia tree in a tiny courtyard, grazing our way through a five-course meal. I was always surprised how a huge terrine could be set in front of you to dig in for as much as you liked, with the ever present basket of gorgeous French bread and the bottle of dubious red wine.

There were several English people who lived there permanently and others, like us, who came and went. The nearest neighbour to my side was memorable, in that she taught me that when I planted anything like a bougainvillea, I must say *Merde, merde merde* (i.e. shit x three) as apparently it helps it to grow!

But the one neighbour who featured most prominently was the elderly farmer, M. Nadaud. He owned three properties round and about, that we knew of. His wife had died some years ago of cancer and he lived in a very basic way with his aged mother. We came to know him because of the need for big ladders. The old house was covered in ivy, which every year had to be cut back to stop it intruding into the roof. It looks lovely but is incredibly destructive as it gets under the pantiles and lifts them off and it's pretty harsh at eating into the mortar on the walls. So every year the season would begin with the words *Est-ce-que nous pouvons emprunter vos echelles,* which he kindly let us do.

They lived very simply inside the house, with no running water indoors, so he used to wash in the tap in the sink in the yard and we didn't enquire as to the other facilities. Tablecloths consisted of sheets of newspaper spread out on the table, everything done most meticulously.

It was probably in our second year that it became apparent that the old lady, who was about ninety-seven, was dying. She had a bed installed on the ground floor and we were invited to go and sit round it and to have a drink.

We knew how to enjoy ourselves! Every so often she would need to be turned and Paul was enlisted to help with this operation, which brought forth the most heart-rending wail from her, which M. Nadaud instructed us to ignore. Several days passed thus and finally she too. It was, we felt, quite an honour to be included in such intimate moments and it certainly created a very strong bond between us. Partly, I suspect he was quite lonely apart from one relative who was there to support him.

He was particularly proud of the liquors he used to make from the fruit he grew. Along the top of the wall of his garden there stood row of little bottles of various coloured liquids – cassis was my absolute favourite. I can't remember – if I ever knew – the reason for them standing there. But every year on the eve of our departure *le depart* he would invite us over to partake, at the kitchen table, of that year's produce. It amused him immensely when he encouraged me to try a clear liquid, which turned out to be *eau de vie* neat alcohol, and he watched my reaction.

So we would toast the end of another year and he would always get emotional and with tears in his eyes would say *Vous me laissez tout seul dans mon petit coin du village*. And I believe that with all his Gallic air of depression, he was in his way genuinely fond of us. He certainly contributed to helping us furnish our vast, empty ruin, supplying us with the bottom half of a buffet which had seen better days but served as our kitchen cupboard. Also, one day there appeared on his tractor and trailer an old traditional French sleigh bed. It looked lovely but was bloody uncomfortable – being only 4ft wide and of a length made for a Hobbit. But it filled the corner of the huge sitting room with a few cushions on it.

Apart from that we had an old double bed and two

bunk beds which we took down and a kitchen table, but that is another story. A rusty ancient frying pan appeared on the day I left, with the note. His dry sense of humour telling me now I had a cooking utensil, he was waiting for an omelette!

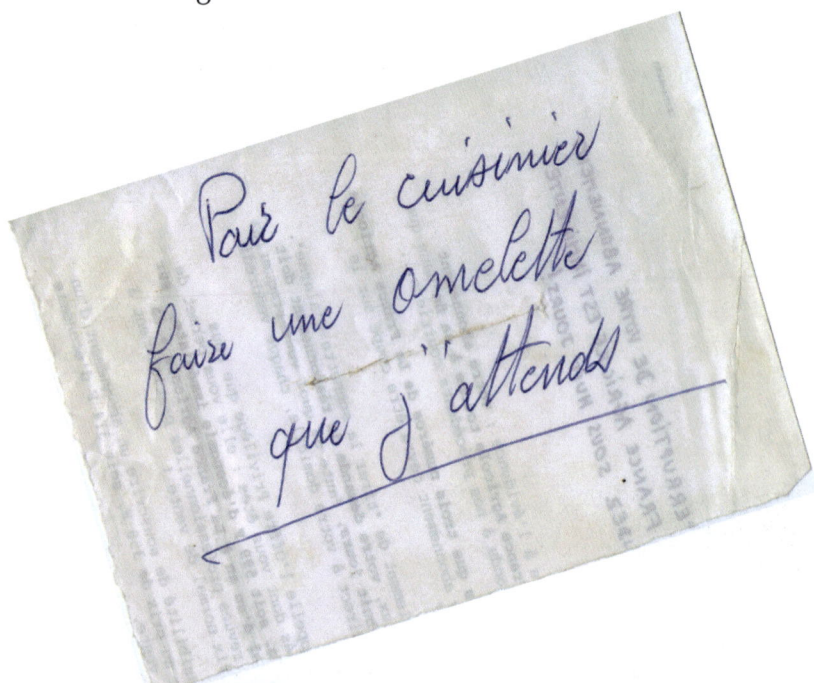

> Pour le cuisinier faire une omelette que j'attends

We reached the point where we could almost move in and camp, but the plumbing and the loo were not yet operational. For some reason, we could not stay at the Rainey's and were wondering how we were going to cope, when M. Nadaud offered to put us up. For a few nights until things were functioning.

That was fine except I had one big problem with that arrangement. The room we were to sleep in was connected to his room, which meant you had to pass through it to go downstairs. Now, I could not get through the night without a pee and could not see how I was going to get through his room, downstairs and out to the loo without disturbing him. So, I figured out that I would claim that Ciaran, who by then was about three, needed a potty in the night.

This I had to use, and if you have ever tried to pee quietly in the middle of the silence of the night into a china chamber pot, you will have some idea how embarrassingly loud and long it was.

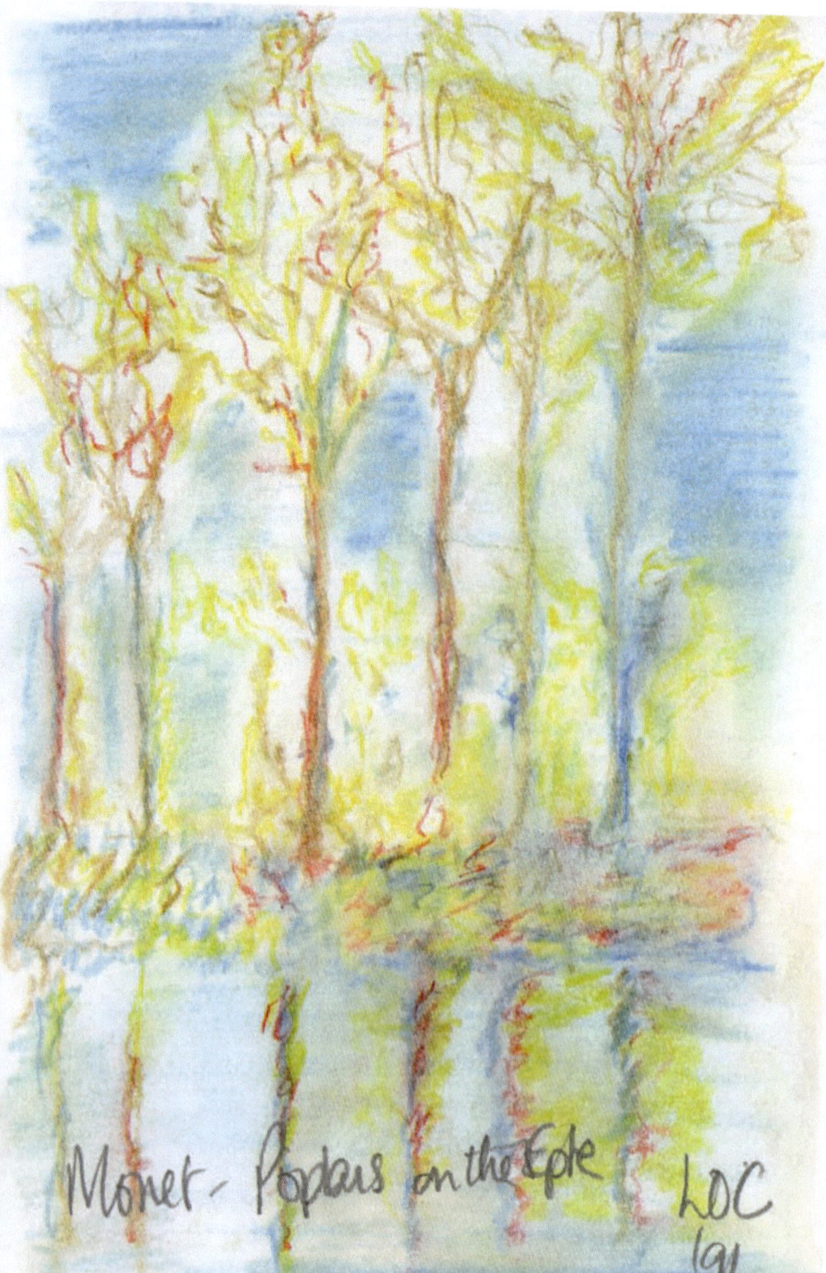
Monet - Poplars on the Epte
LOC
'91

CHAPTER 10

The annual ritual

Thus installed, utterly rustically, we spent the next fourteen summers with the same ritual. The long drive down through the beautiful Loire region, with the magnificent chateaux, the wines, Sancerre, Vouvray, Pouilly Fuisse, noting always with a thrill how the grey slate roof tiles gave way to the warm, inviting hue of terracotta, and how the fields of golden *tournesols* appeared to turn their heads to welcome us back.

The excitement of the arrival was always tinged with a slight anxiety as to what issues/problems would await us. Mostly it would be nothing more worrying than the overgrowth of weeds, dog poo on the drive, the ivy gone rampant and inside the evidence that the mice had had a good winter munching their way through anything available in our very primitive and accessible buffet. One year we had received this beautifully written letter from our neighbour, concerned about the laying of the water supply across the road (see overleaf).

The rhythm of life quickly established itself, a stroll down to the boulanger to buy a baguette or pain au chocolat for my fast-growing boy and the obligatory 'vache qui rit' cheese, or packet of madeleines, which I don't think were a match for those in Proust's *À la recherche du temps perdu*. Then, if it were not to be

NADAUD Maxime   9/12/91
Galles. Lavalette
    16190   Chers Amis
Montmoreau
                C'est avec un grand plaisir que
je reçois votre missive du 30/11. Je suis
complètement seul dans mon fond de bourg aussi
je vous assure que votre venue sera la bienvenue
à tous point de vue. Je ne compte point être
absent en cette fin d'Année.
Par exemple, un problème important pour vous.
Le responsable de la Compagnie des Eaux vous
a coupé l'eau dans la vide, soi-disant qu'il
n'y a pas de règlement de votre part pour
cette fourniture. Voyez ce que vous pouvez
envisager ? faut-il que je m'occupe pour vous
la faire remettre. De toutes façons, vous pourrez
en prendre à la maison en attendant que
cette coupure n'existe plus mais cela ne pourra
vous donner de l'eau chaude. Dans l'attente
que vous preniez une décision, d'être fixé à
ce sujet et surtout de votre venue, veuillez
agréer, M.° M.™° mes plus cordiales salutations
Pour le Bois, pas de problème vous aussi   M. Nadaud

J'ai deux lettres pour vous : une du percepteur de Montmoreau et l'autre pour la Redevance de la Télévision.
Je pense qu'elles peuvent attendre votre venue à Salles ! A bientôt donc.

a working day, packing up lunch and swimwear and off to the river beach at Aubeterre, where we spent so many of our summers under the blue sky, dipping in and out of the river.

I always remember Ciaran asking me one day, 'Mummy, why do your thighs wobble when you walk?' Quel brat! Having been, for several years previously, a Benny Hill Girl, with rather good legs, I was mortified. I came upon a competition – and I never do competitions, – to win slimming treatment for thighs. I entered and I explained my story and I WON! I needed the treatment. It was great for a month or two but there was no way I could continue paying for it so frobby thighs soon returned. Now I always think of Thora Hird in Alan Bennett's *Cream Crackers under the settee*, as a widow living at home alone, looking down at her legs and exclaiming 'Is them my legs? Them's never my legs' and I totally relate.

We did everything on a shoestring financially. Ciaran had a little inflatable paddling pool in the garden. The great drawback with the house, which would always prevent it from being done up in some grand manner at great cost, was its position. It sat, facing the cottage, in the drive which was shared, so it was rather hemmed in. The garden, such as it was, very small and mostly a gravel drive round the north side and some rough grass, which had to scythed annually.

One year, with great pride we bought him a set of swings – hung from a large green tubular frame which was very popular for the kids in French gardens. Then came the bike! As he grew to about seven it became obvious he had need of one. It was a gloriously safe area for kids to roam around, in quiet lanes with virtually no traffic. I sold a Victorian brass hall light and raised the money to buy a small, bright green bike on which he hurtled around the village. He made friends with two little local girls, Laetitia and Aurelie, and a rather dashing young Gallic lad, who lived a little further away, and best of all with a little English girl called Hannah. The two of them spent hours hunting for fossils and collecting stick insects in jars.

My love of the French language grew exponentially. I used every opportunity I had to improve it. Thinking back, I absorbed a lot from reading billboards and signs on the roads as we travelled and explored, *un train peut cacher un autre, Defense de fumer, pelouse interdit* etc. etc – all built in over the years. But oh so often I did not get it right! Quel faux pas I made, so often, like in the States when you ask for a rubber!

We made friends with a couple from Paris. He was particularly dishy – probably the only guy I had a bit of a thing for in years – sadly it was totally no go of course. Sorry, nothing fruity here! Just a lovely whimsical idea. I soon learned that French men speak an exuberantly romantic language to convey the most mundane sentiment. One must become aware of this. One evening we were having a drink by the hotel pool where they were staying,

Now, every occasion from a brief encounter at the morning shops to a full blown welcome at a dinner party requires a *bisou* on the cheek, sometimes both cheeks, and here in the Charente/Dordogne even four kisses, one on each cheek and then repeat. I expressed my surprise and amusement to Renais '*Ca m'amuse, comme on fait la baisse quatre fois ici en Dordogne*'. '*Non, non, non* 'replied Renais, his wife trying to hush him up, '*Non*' Lesley must learn. When we got home later I looked it up in my Larousse Dictionary and found that what I had been saying was 'I find it amusing how one f…s, sc…s and lays here, 4 times in the Dordogne'. No wonder he wanted to correct me.

Apart from river swimming, the town of Aubeterre was famous for its underground monolithic cathedral. The first church was dug out of the cliff in the 7th century and enlarged by Benedictine monks in the 12th century. It. was inspired by churches constructed in Turkey from whence was learnt the technique of digging from the top to the bottom. From the entrance one descends into a vast cavern where early persecuted Christians had worshipped. The ground was hollowed out with some 170 open tombs, all facing Jerusalem, in which lay the skeletons of those long gone. There are galleries and walkways hollowed out and nowadays subtly lit. The whole has the semblance of a macabre film set and left an indelible impression.

Pilgrims would come to pray here as part of the Camino de Santiago de Compostela. It was the parish church until 1794 when it became a saltpetre factory to supply gunpowder for the Revolution. It later opened again, becoming a cemetery until it was stopped for health reasons (not for the dead, I take it). Incredibly, a rockfall hid it and it was only rediscovered in 1950s. It is truly spectacular and so worth a detour if in the area.

CHAPTER 11

Going back to the jippy tum

If you remember, a while back I described the unspeakable scene that had taken place in the supermarket car park in Montpellier. As I mentioned then, I was left with a jippy tum, which got slowly worse over the next two years.

I lost weight, began to suffer dreadful headaches which felt like someone was drilling down into my skull. I regularly used to go into chemists and ask them if they had something for the pain in my stomach, which I clutched explaining 'it feels like rats are gnawing my guts'. Yes I did go to the doctors, always with this infection or that, and with the same complaint. They were at a loss with me. 'Take a holiday!' or 'would you like some anti-depressants?' No, I was not suffering from depression, but I soon would be if I can't find out what's wrong.

That summer, while staying in Dorothy's cottage, I picked up a book from her shelf *Dealing with the Reversal Process and the Healing Crisis through Eliminating Diets and Detoxification* by Dr B Jenson. But it was a serendipity moment. As I read I became more and more engrossed. It described exactly the symptoms I was experiencing and attributed them to a poor inner sewage system. The recommendation was to go on a carrot soup diet which would give it a good cleanout.

So that is what I undertook to do. I asked to be taken seriously in this and duly went on this regime for six weeks, eating carrot soup, carrot rappe. No, fortunately I didn't turn orange – that was just my gorgeous sun tan – but perhaps I had and it was disguised!

One morning, back in England, getting up ready to go to school, I had the most horrific shock. Going to the loo, I was suddenly aware of pulling yards and yards of stuff from myself, like a magician pulling endless linked hankies from his pocket. Yards, it went on, it must have been 20 yards, and looking, I instantly recognized it from drawing it in my school biology lessons, years before, as a tapeworm.

I screamed, felt like I had been raped and flushed it down the loo. So no evidence. Over the following week I continued to lose segments, which I took to the doctors. It was sent off for analysis and diagnosed as a beef tapeworm. I thought you could only get them from pork. But no, apparently from beef and white fish! As it had been eliminated from stock in this country, it became evident I had acquired it in France and I knew exactly the time and place and the rare cooked barbecued steak, confirmed timewise by its length.

The doctors had to have a case conference in Cambridge as none of them had ever dealt with this before. They explained that the head would still be latched onto my guts and would regrow. So a dreadful concoction was administered and I had to wait eight hours for the outcome. And my god, it was some outcome. Enough said!

Apparently, I learnt from my osteopath – I had been suffering dreadful spinal pain during this whole time and it has remained with me all the rest of my life – carrot is the one thing that poisons them and that I was so lucky to have happened upon it, as the bloody thing would have gone on gnawing through me to my brain.

The whole sorry saga, coupled by being attacked around my throat by someone who shall remain nameless, left me with terrible symptoms of random, inexplicable pain with which I struggled for fourteen years, thinking I must have a tumour, a blood clot, or be going mad, until I finally got an MRI scan and a diagnosis of fibromyalgia, which has been my constant companion now for the last forty years and with which I have come to terms and put it down to PTSD following these two traumas in my life occurring at around the same time.

CHAPTER 12
The wildlife within

The thing one quickly comes to realise, living in a hot climate, is that there is always a prevalence of wildlife, much of which seems more than happy to share living quarters. Obviously, there is always the constant nuisance of mosquitoes and flies but I soon learnt that that was just the start.

Apart from the luxury of days off down by the river, most of our time, for the first few years, was spent hacking, digging, shovelling rubble and plaster and mixing cement. On one such day, quite early on, I was in the room, which would one day serve as kitchen and living/dining room, breaking up the rubble that had served as the ground floor, wearing the usual cut-off denim shorts and espadrilles, when quite suddenly I felt something warm, furry and large brush past my leg. I screamed, of course. Whatever it was had descended the existing rickety old wooden stairs and run outside. I soon learned from my neighbour that it was a *fouine* or pine martin. It was about the size of a fox with a similar brush tail, and could scale the walls and live up in the *grenier* – the large open attic space under the roof. Years later, I had another one scale the wall of my second floor terrace in my little village house in Provence. The villagers scorned me when I told them, until they too had visitations and admitted *tu as raison*, Lesley.

The intruders I hated, and feared the most, were the hornets (*frelons*). Several times over the years, they nested in the huge *cheminée* and would lurk around the inside of the house. I have always been terrified of them since when living at the Old Forge, my neighbour, when putting on her dressing gown in the night, was stung by one hiding in the sleeve. They have this terrible habit of lurking in curtains, fabric – so dangerous. The poor woman, who was twenty weeks pregnant, suffered a miscarriage as a result of the sting.

So on their arrival that year, as with any crisis in

France, we called the *pompiers* who are not just fire fighters, but kind of medics as well. They seem to arrive to deal with most emergencies. They would duly turn up and having erected a massive system of ladders. which had to stretch from the road to the second storey of the house that itself stood on a bank 6ft from the road, don all their protective gear and mount the huge ladders. Having climbed to the very top of the chimney stack, they then sprayed it to kill the nest. We would then be on red alert for several days. Most would be found lying dead on the floor in the sitting room around the fireplace, but there were always a few dozy ones lurking about.

One such time, Ciaran was in there playing some board game with his two little French friends, when suddenly I spotted a hornet climbing up Aurelie's arm towards her neck. I cannot describe, or explain what happened next, but somehow I transmitted this to Ciaran and like the perfect swat team one of us swiped it and one of us stamped on it. Boom ... it was gone and Aurelie knew nothing and we were a little shaky.

CHAPTER 13

And there was more ...

We finally realised that no matter how we tried to sand and scrub the huge old floorboards upstairs, which we would love to have salvaged, there was no way, they were not viable. So we took a huge breath and forked out to have the whole lot relaid, sadly with pine ... best we could manage. Thus, the excitement of returning the following year to see it for the first time was palpable. It was indeed spectacular, this huge room with its sepulchre-like stone fireplace – looked like some ballet studio. But the joy of seeing it was soon tempered by the sight that was awaiting us. Right in the middle of this wondrous new spectacle was a huge, and I mean huge splat of bird poo that could have only come from an owl (une *chouette*). There had been a barn owl in the bedroom! Now I love owls as much as anyone, and stand for hours in the winter here in Suffolk, hoping to see one pass. In days past they would fly alongside you as you drove. Not anymore. But an owl in my bedroom? No, that was too close for comfort.

Quite quickly I sussed out that the second rickety staircase up to the *grenier* was open at the top and that there was indeed a nest of *chouettes* seated immediately above our head. You could hear the young ones peeping. No way! There was no way I was going to sleep in that room. No, I was off to the nearest whatever, anywhere, unless that stairwell was securely blocked off. Which was done. So I spent a very uneasy summer sharing the old priory with these magnificent birds. They would swoop and dive over our doorway as the evening closed in, in a way that was both awesome and alarming. My French neighbour (not M. Nadaud) declared that *ils sont méchants (wicked),* and that we should call the *pompiers* to get them removed to another location. So yet again I was on to the *pompiers*, who duly arrived a few evenings later with the ladders and all the gear. The chief asked me to pinpoint the location in the rafters where I thought they were nesting. I indicated that I thought the nest was between two huge roof timbers and I warned him to be careful as they were very large. I demonstrated the width of their wingspan. He grunted and pulled his visor down and began his ascent.

The word had soon spread around the small community that there was some excitement going on at the edge of the village and gradually folk appeared carrying their *appéros* all eager for some activity. Meanwhile, the main man was thrashing about with his gloved hands in the ivy at the eaves level. To explain, these old stone buildings were constructed with no roof felt and there was a space right round the top of the wall plate on which the roof rafters were laid at intervals. Partly this was to allow an air current through to keep the timber dry. Also it was an ideal entry point for wildlife, be it *fouines, frelons* or owls.

Very shortly the guy descended and raising his vi-

sor he declared *Il y n'a pas des frelons la*. Aghast at the misunderstanding, I explained it was owls he was looking for, not hornets the size of an Exocet missile. With one typical Gallic *poof* he collected his ladders

and left. So the owls remained and departed on their own terms, and now in these days when so few are to be seen here in Suffolk, I share the regret that D.H. Lawrence felt in his poem *Snake*. As he appreciates the beauty of the departing creature, he regrets his earlier aggression:

> I picked up a clumsy log
> And threw it at the water-trough with a clatter …
> And immediately I regretted it.
> I thought how paltry, how vulgar, what a mean act …
> And so, I missed my chance with one of the lords
> Of life.
> And I have something to expiate:
> A pettiness.

And so like him, I now feel that I should have been honoured that the owls visited us.

Several years later, when Ciaran, who was by then about seven, and I were down at Salles la Valette on our own, we had some visitors that did not make us feel so honoured. Ciaran had gone to bed and I retired to my ballet studio bedroom, which apart from the bed, an old chest of drawers and a hanging rail was without furniture. I settled into my bed with a copy of Laurence Olivier's biography.

Following my passion for horses that started when I was about seven, and has lasted all my life, at about fourteen I became besotted with Olivier. The rest of my class were all listening to Bill Hayley and the Comets – the advent of rock 'n roll, and of course Elvis. I would spend hours drinking in every minute nuance of Olivier's delivery of Henry V, Hamlet and then Richard III. Apart from being the genius that he was as an actor, he had received vigorous voice training by Elsie Fogerty at the Central School of Speech Training and Dramatic Art. I was entranced by his vocal range and, being an aspiring performer myself, learnt so much from him.

Back to the bedroom, absorbed in my book I slowly became aware of a humming which grew into a buzzing which reached alarming levels. Meanwhile, the room was becoming even darker and the noise was increasing. It was an invasion. Presumably from down the *cheminée* hundreds and hundreds of flies had appeared. It was like a Hitchcock movie. I began frantically swotting them. Ciaran appeared to find out what was going on and I shouted for him to get the hoover. Literally as fast as we cleared the floor of one lot it was again covered. Quite gross! Apparently, they are cluster flies that swarm seasonally in old houses. Since then I have lived in two timber-frame houses with them, but fortunately always in the attic. In fact, this past weekend we had them arrive in an attic bedroom in our present home.

After that, you would probably think, 'what else?' Well, there was one small visitation in the night. I had a small bean bag over my eyes to relax a tremor I was suffering. I had left the book aside on my bed and fallen asleep with the little bag of linseeds on my eyes. In the morning, I awoke to find the bag with a small hole gnawed in it and the linseeds scattered on the pillow. I had had a little visitor in the night – a mouse?

CHAPTER 14

Seventeen years and the big rift

Without going into any gory details, twenty-one years after it had begun, my second marriage crashed. OK, so I am not very good at choosing a partner – I really do think I am quite good at being married but not necessarily to the right guy. At the time, it was following the 1989 property crash, before which we had put our home up as collateral to borrow for business. Bad idea. We had, as we had been told to, 'got on our bikes'. The first venture, a barn conversion, was a success and, high on adrenaline, we had bought two more. God – what a nightmare. Nothing moved, nothing shifted – we couldn't even sell our lovely home to reduce the debt with interest rates now at 17%. People around were committing suicide in financial despair. I took a job at a convent school – it was bliss but it closed nine months later. My other half had nothing. I took another job in an 'enlightened' state school to teach drama for three hour-periods to classes of 45 students ages fiteen to sixteen, half of whom were on remand, some for rape.

I stuck it out, meanwhile our lovely home sold, having devalued by buckets and we moved lock, stock and every log of wood into one of our completed and unsold barns. By this time, I admit that I felt like a rat in a trap. The classes, to all intents and purposes, looked to be working but they were completely annihilating any last vestige of my coping mechanisms. I came the nearest ever to a total nervous breakdown. I could barely speak. Dosed on lorazepam, I was offered yet another contract at another secondary school. At that time, the barn we were living in sold and so we ended up living in a caravan on a very meagre plot with another barn for us to convert bit by bit. My new job, I embraced with every fibre of my being. I liked the ethos; determined, I mounted a small school production – having done several in the past. I returned to acting in the evenings at the Maddermarket Theatre playing Jeanette, the lady in *The Lady's not for burning'* – an incredibly demanding part. Fry's verse, unlike Shakespeare, is horribly difficult to learn.

Buoyed up by hitting fifty, and determined to be a survivor, I then played Elizabeth in Richard III. Wonderful duologue, utter verbal rapier play. Quite suddenly, I was struck by massive panic attacks from which I had never before suffered. Terrifying black space in front of you and no words will come. And then I couldn't get the words out sharp enough. I decided it was the bloody lorazepam that was slowing my verbal response so I just stopped taking it. NEVER do that! Following the get-out, let me explain, it's when everybody, stage hands and actors spend the days dismantling the set, then teaching five days a week, one is performing six nights a week plus matinee for ten days. Exhausting doesn't come into it. As I said, following the get-out on the Sunday, I suddenly could not see the road ahead, when driving. I was forced to tilt my head back and look down my nose to see the road.

Suffice to say, this got worse throughout eighteen months of total terror. I had just been given a full-time teaching contract, was the only wage earner, co-owner of a partially developed barn rhat we had managed to buy while living in a caravan and, getting the kids to read their work out to me, quite suddenly my eyes would not work. The lids kept closing which was diagnosed as a blepharospasm (uncontrollable eye twitching that forces your eyes closed) and my ability to focus had gone to pot. No one knew why. No one knew what to do. I sat in utter despair.

For a while I managed getting lifts to and from school, but eventually I had to concede that I could not cope. A very dear friend who had heard of my predicament arranged for me to see a Dr Sharma in Harley Street. and offered to pay. I went into the clinic for a week and really can attest that beetles crawl over the walls at night with withdrawal. After six months of support my sight slowly returned. Lovely man that he was and still is, he said the bill was in his drawer and as far as he was concerned it could stay there. I did get my sight back, retained my job and over a period of time was able to repay him.

When separation came, there was precious little to separate. The house in France was valued at about £20,000. It was about a third of our remaining assets so my ex took that and the remainder was split between my son and I. Primitive as it was, my husband made it his home and has lived a kind of boho/hobo life there ever since.

The divorce, acrimonious to say the least, took over two yrs and before I lost all rights to it I wanted to get my stuff – not a lot, a few clothes, couple of rugs and painting of a sunflower, which I had bought off an Australian artist, who was painting on the beach one day. The painting was and still is a great big splash of joy to me, so vibrant and evoking such memories of the fields full of 'tournesols', so much part of the Charentais landscape.

So I arranged for a friend to drive me down on a fast four day turnaround trip, very mindful of funds, booked us into a very 1* pension. It was very much low season, in fact no season at all. And this was rough. While in the shower I noticed a large beetle-like thing crawling up the wall. Later I saw more of these things. I couldn't identify them but one crawled across the bed. It was a while later, at a dinner party, that my friend pointed out to me that they had indeed been cockroaches! It just keeps on getting better, doesn't it?

Anyway, on a foggy, damp morning I made a discreet and very fast visit to the old house and picked up my things to take the road back, only to find that the French tanker drivers were on strike and finding fuel to get back to school for Monday was a sweat. Another time the farmers had mounted a protest (they are so into that there) whereby during the night, every signpost was covered with glued-on newspaper for miles and miles. So that was the end of my time at the house that I had had for the longest and where my boy had grown from a child into a young man.

Ciaran and I say farewell to Le Prieuré…

CHAPTER 15

Transitioning

Not, I hasten to add, in the currently fashionable sense, more passing from one phase of life to another, with great uncertainty, moving through a kind of limbo, and then maybe clutching at a life raft. Anyhow, after a couple of years being single with a now nearly grown-up son, and still teaching fulltime to A level, I drifted into a relationship with an old family friend, who was then on his own. Seems to be the pattern of my life. So, I opted for pallid and provincial, hey, but secure! No Francophile, he. But he was desperate to spend his hard-earned money on a yacht and retire.

OK … it seemed a pleasant enough plan. Turkey was his first thought – a mooring there perhaps? No, that was tried, loved the food, and rejected. Spain? How about the South of France, I tentatively suggested. The mind, quietly dreaming and scheming – a mooring – visits to a boulangerie, local brasseries, French restaurants. I certainly saw the possibility here of retaining some of my lost passion.

A visit was proposed. A drive down to the Med. Not to stay on the coast as I knew we would be gridlocked in summer but a radial point. I selected Les Arcs sur Agen. Brilliant. A wonderful hotel and daily sorties down to various different points along the coast that offered the possibility of moorings. One such trip took us through the village of La Garde Freinet (LGF). This village stood about 12 miles back from St Tropez back up in to the Jura Mountains, where it had in times past obviously been a sentry point as there were amazing ruins of an earlier Moorish settlement in the mountain overlooking the village. Passing through LGF I was bowled over by this scenic, bustling village.

On the pavement was the overspill from a shop selling large, painted wooden animals. STOP! STOP! I had to explore. The large wooden chicken I had to buy. In so doing, with my reasonable French, I got into conversation with the colourful, extremely crazy proprietress, Josianne. She who was to feature so much in the next ten plus years of my life. I loved the village. Were we looking to buy? That was not the plan. She knew just the place! (On commission? Oh yes.) I returned to the car with the chicken and an appointment to view an old house here in the village tomorrow. The idea was not rejected.

We went, we saw, we bought. A tiny, utterly bijou four storey village house. It was probably the first time in my life I had ever been tempted to buy something that was not a pile of rubble. The matter was not discussed on the two-day drive home. Then I proposed that I could pay for half of it and it would give me a home. Surprisingly, the suggestion was met with approval and hey presto we decided to buy it, and also settle on a nearby mooring at Cogolin for the boat he was to buy. Thus began the final twelve year stage of my deep love affair with France.

We travelled down in late October to complete. I remember, I had bought myself a beautiful Jaeger camel coat for the occasion – I still have it, some twenty-five years later and it is still beautiful. Var, the region, the department of Provence we were entering, has the highest level of sunshine in the area but not that October. It rained, oh how it rained, stair rods, cats and dogs, *les chats et les chiens* interminably, for days and days. We had hired a trailer to take down a load of furniture, surplus at home, with which to start to furnish the little house. Problems were: 1. We couldn't get the trailer up the narrow street. 2. We couldn't get anything up the tiny winding stone staircase to the living floor. We needed two strong guys to lug it up the street, and then with webbing straps to heave it up over the first-floor terrace into the place.

But a greater problem overriding all was, we couldn't get in! The key did not open the door. This all in all was not a promising start. So a locksmith was duly summoned (when he had the time) and locks were changed. The biggest problem solved, then the other three, and we were in, and still it was pissing down.

Then we discovered that the trailer, which we had parked in a car park outside the village, had been stolen. Boy, it was getting better and better. But hang on a minute … there was more. Visiting the supermarket, my reluctant partner stepped in the biggest piece of dog shit, only realizing when he got into the car. I won't go into further details, but all in all, torrential rain, burglary, eternal dog shit, one of the things I most hated about France, all this was not an auspicious welcome to our new home and did little to convince my somewhat reluctant partner to a love of France.

CHAPTER 16

Never mind the Bayeux … the tapestry that was La Garde Freinet

In my wildest dreams and in my most crazy imagination I could not have envisaged the extraordinary, colour, variety and magic of that tiny mountain village. Situated under a lowering mountain to the north side, topped with a massive crucifix of Christ overseeing all. And along the ridge, as I have mentioned, the remains of a Moorish settlement, all the walls and rooms still evident among the rosemary and lavender. The crucible of civilisations was warring then and struggling to amalgamate now in the 21st century. It was peopled with characters straight out of a cartoon book.

The 'chicken lady' Josianne, who I have already mentioned, became very attached. She hailed from Paris originally, and had been a film costume designer in times past, and the story went that she had been run out of Paris by gunmen and had not stopped running running running until she reached LGF. Among her many qualities, she had the most amazing pair of boobs, which she revelled in flashing publicly and often. I don't think this was a particularly French trait. Perhaps she was a stripper in a former life. I have to say I took most of her stories with a large pinch of salt but she was indeed prone to dramas. Anyway in La Garde Frienet, here she made her home, in a tiny flat above a shop in the market square. It was a little haven of eccentric creativity and the most marvellous food. I learnt so many tips for cooking from her. She seemed honoured to have me as a friend, the English lady who was a 'prof'. School teachers are/were so much more socially valued there than here. She corrected my French continuously and told me to stop speaking academic French and learn some *argot*. When she banged on my door one morning before 10am and started correcting me – I drew the line. Before 10am and after 10pm, I could muddle my tenses, mix up masculine and feminine forms and she was *inderdit* to correct me!

We shared sons both called Tristan, although mine rarely spoke to me, hers did. He lived next door and sported an 8ft iguana, which, when not in its glass case, would be draped around his neck as he walked the streets, accompanied by his pitbull dog, which I did not like and was forbidden to come into my house. Her partner, Ness, who she subsequently married and at whose marriage I was witness, was a Sicilean with a heart of gold and a temper that could be heard all over the pantiled rooftops of the village. His brother was something else – a true fully muscled Sicilian mafioso who rode a magnificent grey stallion bareback through the village. He was someone I kept well clear of.

As with so many villages, it had its twice weekly market, which apart from the produce was the heart of the community, meeting for coffee or a pastis. When you ordered a bouquet from the florist stall, they would engineer a beautiful arrangement and deck it in wrappings and ribbons with little regard to the time it took or the queue of waiting customers.

It was the village of festivals. In the summer was the *soupe au pistou*, a soup made by the villagers, me included, whereby tons of and tons of fresh vegetables were delivered to the Salle de Fête and chopped up to create this special soup, which was then served with slow roasted pork and all the trimmings on long trestle tables in the street, mistral permitting. In the autumn there was the chestnut festival. The surrounding Massif des Maures mountains were covered by the beautiful, distinctive *pins parasols*, cork oak trees and by huge grand sweet chestnut trees, sadly many of which were dying and some ravaged by the summer wildfires. So chestnut products would fill all the many stalls, from ice cream to confitures or simply chestnuts roasting in braziers all around, emitting that unmistakable inviting smell.

The butcher was a speciality! Jean Jacques supplied superb delicatessen and meat, but was and still is an opera singer. So our singing butcher entertains his customers who sit on benches in his shop awaiting their turn whilst listening to an aria. And, oh my, who those customers were – the great and the famous. The walls are covered in signed photographs of all the stars and celebrities who are his regular customers.

And the village certainly attracted many celebrities to live there or at least have second homes there. The Redgraves, Liam Nielsen and Alan Rickman (now deceased), could be seen regularly in the local cafés and bars. Le Faucado, the most famous of the restaurants, was also a big draw. There you could sit and dine in one of the prettiest walled gardens shaded by bougainvillea and wisteria dripping off metal trellis arches. Down in the beach restaurants, one would find oneself sitting next to a very discreet and elderly but still beautiful Brigitte Bardot.

The one little thing that really touched my heart was that under the window off my first floor kitchen, I could look out and see, sitting below me, three or four *barvardeurs*, the old ladies from the village in their black garb, knitting, crocheting, sewing and chatting away to each other peacefully. They would wave up to me calling out *Faites des beaux reves* Lesley. Sweet dreams! How lovely was the sheer simplicity, honesty and warmth of that greeting and how soothing the quiet, gentle chatter.

CHAPTER 17

La canicule, 2003

Spending many weeks there, we soon came to realise that we needed some outside space. Our tiny village house afforded us only a very small roof terrace, limited sunlight and room only for the most modest entertainment or BBQ. We decided we needed to move. There was quite literally virtually nowhere within the village to move to that would have suited our needs. The forest that surrounded it was dotted with gorgeous properties with swimming pools and space that was very enticing. But the threat of burglary out there was very real, no matter how sophisticated an alarm system was fitted. That gave us pause. But what really stopped us in our tracks was witnessing the forest fires.

A constant worry all through the summer the heat at 36° plus for several weeks on end, and the mistral often tearing through randomly, with windspeeds of 75mph plus. These fires would literally jump fields, the wind would hurl lighted pine cones like medieval weapons across areas of scrubland and forest, destroying properties and wildlife, jump across roads and motorways leaving a charred and blackened landscape in their wake. It's easy to understand how every property owner in the forest is required to clear the scrubland within 30 metres of its buildings in order to create a *debruossaillage* (clearing). It is the only way to create a firebreak. And it's also the reason why the *pompiers* were on constant fire watch, positioned all around the forest walks to stop some idiot chucking a cigarette butt down.

The year 2003 was known as *La Canicule* – the year of the scorching heat. What an experience! We stood on our roof terrace and looked out at the mountain and alongside us which was literally a blaze of fire like some horror movie. Everyone was packed with essentials ready to evacuate, but we soon learned we were trapped. All roads in and out of the village were cut off. An English couple trying to leave their property were burnt to death.

Helicopters were toing and froing constantly overhead. The Canadair planes swept down across the sea sucking up water and then flew back desperately in an attempt to douse the blaze. Our great saving grace were the *pompiers* – the brave firefighters who were stationed in our village to keep us safe. At one point we had 2,000 of them in the village who had been drafted from Paris and from Italy in a desperate attempt to subdue these terrible fires. The villagers loved them, housed them, fed them and brought them endless coffees and pastis. We owed our lives to them, 15,000 people died in France that fortnight from fires or from the heat.

That most sobering of experiences led us to one conclusion. We had to find somewhere in the village to relocate to. We learned of a small site on the ruins of an old cork factory (the cork oaks had once been the centre of a thriving industry providing the corks for wine bottles) but no more. This site led off the back and sides of two existing old properties with a small area of plateau and down a sheer rock face into an area below which was a triangle of land between two tiny mountain roads leading up to le Criox. We bought it and designed a property that would work on three levels, at the top an entrance and living area with a large terrace, then down a level to two bedrooms and bathrooms and a small terrace, and down again to the third (bottom) floor with a bedroom, bathroom, lower entrance and walled, gated car park. My partner was a structural engineer and I was an interior designer with a reasonable command of French.

We hired the services of a recommended architect

and project manager, M. Dufour. Oh it started so well! All materials possible were sourced from reclaim yards. Exploring round such places was a dream for me. Days spent in the Var, travelling around accompanied by him, to find old beams, beautiful panelled doors, iron railings for the *garde corps* and a magnificent stone *cheminée* for the main room. The windows and shutters would be purpose made, and the pammets for the floor bought new. I have always loved rooting around antique shops, bric-a-bracs and *brocantes*, and here with a reason and for the first time with the money and guidance to indulge it in this way for a purpose was magic.

There were huge issues with the terracing. Because the roads were so steep and narrow, the digger drivers could not access the plot. So they walked off the job. Finally, having resolved that issue, we got started and work got underway. Then our next blow hit. Our project manager had a midlife crisis and bunked off up north with a young lover. *'Alors quoi faire?'* His son Daniel who was but the accountant had to quickly step up and take over and my French had to very quickly get into gear, with daily emails to keep up to date when we were back in England and keep the work progressing.

I guess it was about two years in all, the project, but when it was finished, it was stunning. The interiors on the main floor had very high ceilings so they were all lime brushed, sealed in a beautiful ochre, creams or pastel shades and the dado rail was hand painted, mirrored by a similar rail at picture height level, all

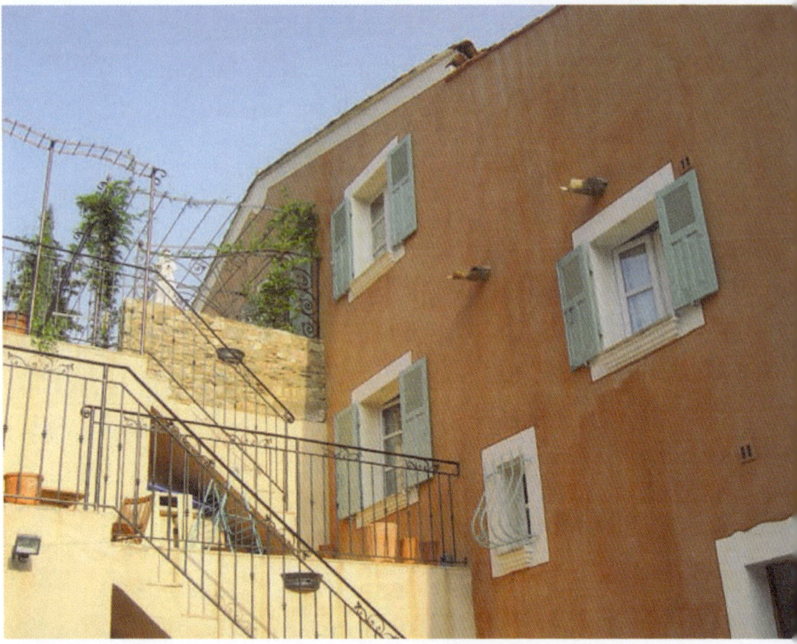

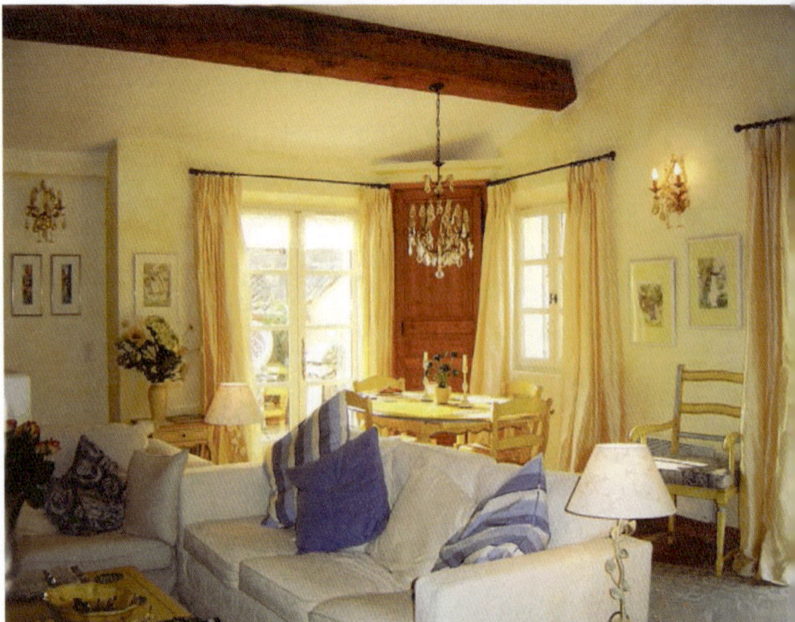

stencilled by a local artist, Gerard. The shower rooms were tiled throughout in small Italian ceramics, one blue/green, and the other peach/pink. The staircase, which was winding and open one side had a plastered balustrade on the other, again stencilled.

Outside a *treille* had been constructed in dull metal work which carried four wisteria and very quickly provided a dappled, shady outside sitting area on the main terrace. The garden, small but utterly charming, surrounded with old walls, was given the ultimate finishing touch of an 100-year-old olive tree which we had craned in and surrounded by lavender. It was in every way a resounding success.

CHAPTER 18

Love France, pity about the French!

I was on my way to Florida (don't bother) when a passenger got talking to me and I was whittling on about France and this is what he said, 'love France, pity about the French'. And I have heard other people say the same. Maybe they are an acquired taste! They have such a fierce sense of their own identity and a pride in their culture: *Liberté, Egalité, Fraternité*. Which is perhaps why they don't readily absorb the immigrant population who don't make an effort to integrate. It's one of the reasons I love them. At times depressive, others exuberant, always very wordy, one of the benefits of philosophy being part of their school curriculum. Often truculent, extremely ready to protest but for the most part they live life with a passion, which is both equal in its depression and its enthusiasm. I do admit that the Parisiens are something else. They cultivate a *froideur* which is neither so engaging or appealing.

If I may say, that I made friends with a Parisian lady, of *une certain age*, Mme Claude, who spent her summer at her residence in La Garde Freinet. You will need to interpret that, as she made friends with me! I think she thought I was worth the trouble of cultivating, or maybe she had just exhausted all the French who had any time for her. On occasions she would invite me to join her for lunch, often at the beach, which was always a lovely experience. One time, four of us were at table and found ourselves seated next to a table with a mother and some French children. Normally, the behaviour of young children in France in restaurants is exemplary. They, like Spanish children, are brought up to behave, unlike, sadly, the appalling behaviour often displayed by British kids. No political correctness here. Madame rounded on the mother and in no uncertain terms made it clear that this was unacceptable, and there was peace! Imagine trying that here.

Recently, I was lunching with a friend in Walberswick and noted that there was a table with two delightfully looking two-four year olds. During our lunch, one of them started screaming her lungs out for a full fifteen minutes and the mother did not remove her from the table. All of the guests eating were visibly disturbed and the proprietor did nothing. We endured it. That is, apart from a Portuguese waiter who in true Latin manner wrung his hands in despair, saying to us that such behaviour would not have been tolerated in his society.

It was the same Madame Claude, who invited me to lunch at the Facaudo and when I arrived, asked why I was alone when the invitation had been extended to *vous*, that is, to include my partner, not simply *tu* the singular version, and surely I knew the difference. She always sat with her little handbag-size dog on her lap, declaring that now she avoided any top Parisian restaurants that would not admit her dog! It was by her that I was scolded for cutting cheese incorrectly. As ever the wondrous cheese board would appear at the end of the meal and she lectured never to cut across the pointed end of the cheese. *Il ne faut pas couper le nez du fromage*. One must never cut the nose off the cheese! My step-granddaughter Abi delights in this story and has ever since insisted on this with her guests.

When I reached the age of sixty, my ten years younger sister, someone I had learned to steer clear of, approached me and said pitifully that she had never been to Paris and would I take her? With some trepidation I agreed and we boarded the TGV and arrived in the Gare du Nord. It was May and very cold. That evening, preparing to go out to a restaurant, she showed me the short, white leather hot pants she was going to wear. I could feel my stomach knotting. She managed to spill the wine and engage four men on the next table, and I counted myself lucky that we got back to the hotel just the two of us. She spoke no French, so I tried to speak discreetly so as not to make her feel uncomfortable. On the morning of our departure, taking coffee and a croissant in a nearby bar, she said she wanted to buy her 200 Silk Cut fags. I offered to do the purchase but she marched up to the bar and in loud English demanded 200 Silk Cut. The bartender looked at her, raised his shoulders in typical Gallic manner and, with an utterance of exasperation, walked away. 'SO rude!', she exclaimed as she came back to me. 'No,' I explained, it is you who are being rude. You never enter a shop or a transaction without an opening 'Bonjour Monsieur/dame'. And that is the same all over France. It is etiquette.

And finally the iceman cometh! One of my favourite moments in France. We were visiting Sète for the night, the delightful small fishing village on the Bay where all the mussels are grown on ropes. The weather was pretty much as usual, beautiful. It was an idyllic waterside scene, the world and his wife promenading, sipping their *apéros*. We were sat in the grounds of the small waterside hotel. There was the usual peaceful buzz that accompanies that drowsy, appreciative moment in the day when the sun is losing its fierceness and a mellow tranquillity has descended. A fisherman or two were trading from their small stalls along the quayside. Quite suddenly, the calm was ripped apart by a youth on a motor scooter, racing through the town emitting the maximum noise he could. A gospel went up all round one to another. What effrontery! *Quel idiot!* The indignation soon gave way to return to the chatting and sipping. Yet wait! Back he came again from the other direction, determined to stamp his aggression on the evening. Well, there was a positive ripple of indignation that passed through all the bystanders and when he tried it for the third time at full throttle, one of the fishermen was waiting for him with a large bucket of iced water and chucked it all over him. Bullseye! The crowd cheered. He wobbled a bit on his scooter and wobbled off with his sad life to try and find someone else to annoy. Or maybe not. Maybe, just maybe he had learned a little lesson. Wonderful. Can you imagine that kind of common-sense, hands-on reaction happening in our country today. I think not.

And you either love them or hate them. And mostly I love them, although I will say, having spent many years living there that the one thing that they lack which I missed the most was the ability to laugh at themselves. They truly lack a sense of self-irony. That was the one main quality that I missed about the English. We are really able to take the mickey out of ourselves and they are not. Taking the mickey is a tendency I have and I was constantly having to explain to them that I was joking as I saw them about to take offence. Although today, I was mortified to read that as part of their 2024 Olympic Games opening, they featured a parody of Leonardo da Vinci's *Last Supper*, portrayed by a load of drag queens. This made me very sad and as one of my favourite historians, commentator Tim Stanley wrote, even the French are not exempt from the rot that is eroding western culture. Is this the same country that when Notre Dame was burning, people filled the streets of Paris and spontaneously started singing Ave Maria. It still has a deep sense of its heritage roots.

CHAPTER 19

Thank you Benny

During those last years of the wonderful 1960s, back living in England, with my screaming infant and playing amazing roles at the Questors Theatre, Ealing, my appetite to become a professional actress became all-consuming. In those days an Equity card was required to be able to act and getting one was no mean feat. It could be achieved by taking a number of small walk-on parts that were exempted, and building up enough to satisfy the union who would eventually issue one. So any small walk-on parts I was offered, I seized upon.

Having done one such small part on a Bernard Cribbins show at Thames Television (which was just down the road from where we lived in Teddington), I received a phone call the next morning asking me could I get down to the studios immediately. They needed a replacement in *The Benny Hill Show*. 'Well, no,' I started to blab', no babysitter', stop woman think. 'Yes of course I could' (I would somehow resolve my babysitting problems). And so I did. Benny took a shine to me and wrote the enclosed article in the *TV Times* and wrote me into the series and I continued to work on the show for the next three seasons. Not, I hasten to add, as a Hill's Angel dancer but doing the sketches and the runoffs.

TWINKLE, TWINKLE LITTLE STAR

Benny Hill has a word for it

UNDERSTANDABLY Benny H can't get over it. "It was li seeing Dame Sybil Thorndi blasting out on a trumpe Very unexpected, if you kno what I mean."

"Twinkle," he says, "can't cultivated. Either you have or you haven't. Marilyn Mo roe had it, Goldie Hawn has **Sue Bond** and **Lesley Gold** (the girls he was talking abo and who appear with Ben in Wednesday's show) ce tainly have it.

"It's more a showbiz thi than an actress thing," he go on. "A lot of very go actresses wouldn't recogni it if they met it head on."

Apparently, there are vario forms of twinkle. Lesley a Sue twinkle in different way "Lesley is lady-like, she's wh you'd call a fine looking wom and very alluring. My area comedy with her is to pull h down when she gets snooty – do the rough and ready Rom and put her in her place.

How does Benny see t future for Sue and Lesley "The way showbusiness going it's hard to say; yc can't predict anything fc anyone these days. But there always a place for a girl wi twinkle," says Benny Hi

BENNY HILL SHOW at 8.0
EDNESDAY JAN 27 *Thames Television Productio*

J.D. AGENCY
34A, WALPOLE STREET, CHELSEA LONDON S.W.3
TEL. 01-730-4816/9777

He was as brilliantly funny off screen as on, but quite a private person. Well, he was with me as he realised pretty damn quick that I was not up for any hankey pankey. He used to refer to me as Auntie or Mummy Bunny and would courteously omit me from any sketches he thought I would not be comfortable doing. However, when he fell out of favour, as he did big time when Thames sacked him and the feminist movement was in full swing, it was a part of my life that I kept under wraps. Albeit, I knew that having played many major classic roles, I would only be remembered for wearing black stocking tops on *The Benny Hill Show*.

But much joy has it brought me over the years, apart from repeat fees helping out with oil bills. While back in teaching during the 1980s, rampant, uncontrollable year eleven louts became awestruck and biddable pupils, when by chance a rather racy sketch was repeated. I dreaded school the next day, but it was a doddle. After all the 'Cor blimey Miss, that was you, wasn't it?', and a curt order, get back into line and go to your places, they behaved like lambs for the rest of the year.

But perhaps one of the most joyous moments resulting from my association with Benny came to me most unexpectedly in a medical setting. My aforementioned crazy friend Josianne was very concerned about the gastric problems I suffered – among others. She insisted I went to see a specialist at St Raphael. So I was finally persuaded to make an appointment. It would be necessary to have both a gastroscopy camera down and a colonoscopy camera up. Not a pleasant prospect. I have never got over having to be stomach pumped after a hospital meal, because I was losing the placenta, and my eight-month-old fetus would die if they did not do an emergency Caesarean section. So this was NOT a pleasant prospect except that in France, they give you an anaesthetic.

Having undergone the extremely unpleasant preparation for the latter … any one who has will know what I mean … it was all quite bearable. I awoke in a ward, with two other French women who were bragging they had had three polyps found, 'Mais moi' I said 'J'ai eu cinq polyps!' I said. Fortunately, they were, at that time, all benign.

They are very hot on those checks being done regularly in France, so over the years I think I underwent three. The final time, I turned up at the clinic in St Raphael to make an appointment to see the anaesthetist. Oh, but I have forgotten to mention, the clinic was run by nuns in full white habits but I hasten to add that the surgery was not performed by them.

On this particular occasion, when I presented myself at the reception desk, I was greeted by several of these nuns with a chorus of *'Oh, c'est Mme* Benny Hill'. I could not believe my ears. It appears that his shows were still popular down in the South of France and particularly with the nuns! And to this day I do not know how they knew of my connection. Following that I went up to meet the anaesthetist, a very dishy, bronzed guy in shorts who also exclaimed the same. This had obviously got round the convent grapevine. I am not quite sure what it says about the mores of that era, when Benny was taboo here and yet so fondly regarded there. Certainly, it would seem that the religious fraternity was less politically correct than the media et al. here in the UK.

On the morning of the 'do', I presented myself, drained and well flushed out as required, at 6am for prep. However, the anaesthetist was not the snazzy, young, tanned guy. This was perhaps an Algerian, certainly not warm and humorous who told me to 'make a fist'. He regarded me, pallid, no makeup, and bedecked in that theatre gown and bonnet and said 'Hmm you don't look much like a Benny Hill girl!' To which I tartly replied, 'Aged nearly 60, at 6am in the morning, having spent the night on the loo and in this get up. What do you expect?'.

But joy very soon returned because as I was wheeled, drowsy from the pre-med, into the operating theatre all the nurses pushing the trolley and those at the doors started singing the Benny Hill tune 'Diddle diddle dum, diddle diddle dum', the runoff theme tune he always used. I will always remember with huge gratitude the joy of that crazy moment and how it so lightened an otherwise dark one.

CHAPTER 20

And that's life

There are, if you are really lucky, some fusion moments when events collide, coincide and spiral you upwards, sideways, all ways and it seems as though you are having a multisensory experience of the essence of being alive. Alternatively, they can be the very opposite when one is hit with a tsunami of grief and despair and 'pitched past pitch of grief' (Gerard Manley Hopkins). Or they can be a mixture of the two. And such an occasion happened to me.

Events took place over a couple of days in 2009. I was at a party at a neighbour, in the village, an elderly bloke with a young, very dishy, bipolar ex rent-boy living in … who knew not only how to spend his partner's money on exquisite shoes but also played the piano divinely. Very drunk, very sexy, he shared the news that the vineyard across the mountain was now an equestrian centre. He was crazy about horses and horsemanship and badgered, nay, forced me into agreeing to go riding with him the next day. All my protestations, that I could no longer ride because of the fibromyalgia, plus I had no gear, were rapidly dissolved. I found myself limping home, very much the worse for drink, wearing a pair of jodhpurs under my skirt and carting a riding hat.

We were to be there by 7am because of the heat. He was to pick me up for the notoriously dangerous mountain drive. So what I ask you, could I do? I rose very early; the alcohol having worn off with the sheer terror of what I had let myself in for. Switching on the radio, my feelings were immediately diverted. The news came through of the death of Michael Jackson. Whatever your opinion of the guy's personal life he was an amazing artist, musician, dancer and I was a huge fan. So, with that filtering through my brain and my emotions, I set off for the immediate challenge.

Apart from being totally terrifying and incredibly difficult and painful to be astride a beautiful grey (my horse had been a grey and they have always been my favourite colour, the dappled ones), the whole experience was so life enhancing. We rode together several times, I was bolted with once and stayed on, clambered up and down the mountainous terrain, with huge boulders to the left and more huge boulders to the right, any one of which would have been lethal on contact – I took back, for a short while one of the greatest joys of my life.

That evening, back home I painted a picture of Michael dancing in *Remember the time*. It was the only way I knew how to deal with the pain of his death. My tiny and not very brilliant tribute. I am happy we seemed to have got over the need to cancel him as a musician, and are again being treated to hearing some of his amazing numbers. If you have never watched the video *This is it*, which tracked the incredible talent and discipline that went into designing his last tour, which sadly he did not make, I urge you to watch it, if you can get past the crutch clutching. It is stunning.

On that musical note, I pass on to the other moment that touched my heart so deeply. Many, many years previously, in another life, I was entranced by the songs and lyrics of Leonard Cohen. Oh yes, I know he can drone on, often in a deeply melancholic tone, but it does hit the spot! And he can also deliver some magical poetry with marvellous jazz backing, that is his own unique style. Well, what with one thing and another, babies, goats and rubble, music had tended to drop out of my life. Then one evening within a day or two of the other events, we were dining with friends just outside LGF when quite suddenly I heard the voice of Leonard Cohen singing *Alleluia*. The response was instant and overwhelming. To everyone's surprise I burst into tears. I waffled something along the lines of how a piece of music can take you back to a time in your life and an intense emotion. 'Oh', they said, 'We're going to hear him tomorrow night, in the olive groves in Nice. We've got a spare ticket if you'd like to come.'

Manna from heaven doesn't fall from the skies like that very often! Boy, I was so thrilled. Off I went with them and we sat on the grass, some perched up in the olive trees on a blissful, warm, calm Provence night, and listened to his now, rich, very bass voice still more than capable of delivery to the delight of the crowd. 'Suzanne', 'The sisters of mercy', 'Bird on the wire', all the old favourites plus plenty that were new. He had a small jazz band and some very sparky backing singers and was still the very man himself, sporting his black trilby hat. Apparently, he had been totally financially ripped off, by his accountant I think and had gone into monastic retreat for several years. Now in his late 70', in the business of sorting out his finances, he was back touring. When he died in 2016, the same year as Bowie and Prince, I was living in Scotland and I lit a candle in my window and mourned the passing of the man wrote 'There is a crack, a crack in everything. That's how the light gets in'.

I arrived back home after the concert at about 1.00am and then had to rise at 6am to return to Nice to board a flight back to Gatwick to be at the funeral of a dear friend Pat, at which I had been asked to speak. Thus for some 48 hours or more I was pitched from pillar to post, emotionally, and physically, overdosed on joy, grief, excitement and totally exhausted 'All passions spent'. But I knew I was alive, and we don't have many days when we can truly say we have been fully 'in the moment' and so many of them, one on top of the other.

CHAPTER 21

Messing about on the water

You may have noticed, that in all this time, I have totally omitted to mention the boat. The purchase of a yacht by my then partner, in his retirement, and the decision to moor it in Cogolin, was the passport that was to give me back a life in France. Thus, it has been very remiss of me. In my defence, messing about in or on the water has never been a passion of mine. Yes, like most kids I enjoyed having fun on the odd pedalo, or on a rowing boat but seriously that was it. And here suddenly, in my mid-fifties I had the challenge of learning to crew a sailing yacht. Do you know what, admitting you have been away, sailing your boat in the Med, has a a certain cachet. It sounds incredibly snobby and entitled, doesn't it? Well, yes, lazing around on deck, in a beautiful marina, sipping a pastis, with the sun setting across the water certainly has its attractions. God, I miss it just thinking about it! I will not deny that I enjoyed those great moments.

This was our boat. A 38ft Dufour, fibreglass craft, called Dolmay. She was beautiful, but for those of you who don't know, a lot of graft, discomfort and hard work is required. There were numerous ropes and knots to learn, fenders to heave up and down, never mind the anchor, which I never touched. Sharing the cabin space, when you have several bods sleeping on the floor, having to tiptoe over them to get to the loo (heads), before returning to an uncomfortable bunk. (Forget Dodi Fayed's yacht that Diana sailed on.) Also halyards clacking all night, trying to cook in a galley (kitchen), and feeling nauseous with the motion of the boat. I won't go on. I am sure I have either won your sympathy, or utterly irritated you.

However, we did have some amazing trips along the legendary Côte d'Azur, stopping in Cassis or Menton, being followed by dolphins, seeing with alarm whales rising out of the water, and in the other direction the amazing formation of the Calanques.

And then the trips across to the Iles of Porquerolles with its turquoise water, forest trails full of Euchalyptus trees, not indigenous, with bark of incredibly subtle colours of slate, turquoise, green, pink. So you know, all in all, it had its moments.

Two things I found difficult when mooring up were first that none of the electrical appliances were compatible, which meant a trip straight away to the capitainerie to buy yet another plug or socket, so we could have power. And the other thing is that everybody shouts a lot. I realise it's important for an order to be relayed clearly from one end of the boat to the other, but so much shouting!

And certainly the boat brought us into contact with many, varied, interesting and occasionally odd folk. Settled in our new mooring in Cogolin, we were pootling about doing jobs on the boat, when an elderly guy in his eighties stood by and started chatting. He had quite a strong Germanic accent and had an appartement in the marina. On hearing that we were from Norfolk, England, he explained his wife too was from there and insisted we come round for an *apéro*. We duly, and somewhat reluctantly agreed as we did not find him appealing company. It was a very uncomfortable affair. The wife hardly spoke and certainly had no interest in meeting us. He was intent on showing us numerous photos of the different properties he owned around the world, never apparently staying very long in any one of them. When we left, we both felt strangely uncomfortable and both noted the total lack of emotional connection in talking about any property. He hailed from South America and had been a surgeon, and the same awful thought struck us. Could he be a Nazi on the run? We made sure we never encountered him again.

The great highlight of the boating season, which I hasten to add, we never took part in, is Les Voiles de Saint-Tropez. Sailboats of all types and sizes from all over the world would moor up in the harbour days before the race, but those that always attracted the greatest attention and excitement were the old classic, wooden, tall ships, some 100 years old and utterly majestic. When the race, originally known as the Nioulargue, began this whole mix of crafts would tack and jibe, In perilous proximity. Sadly, there was a fatal accident and the race was suspended in the late 1990s but is now run again under the title of Les Voiles de Saint-Tropez. Here is the time and place to really experience the real pizazz!

CHAPTER 22

On fine dining or otherwise

Really thought I had made it in life, when during my actressy days, I was invited to make a radio programme for hospitals ... but the excitement was, it involved a trip to France for lunch. For the life of me I can't see why we went to France to do it. Anyway, I thought the occasion demanded a new outfit, having lived almost exclusively in Biba for years, and I can quite clearly remember the olive-green needle cord trouser suit that I bought in the Kings Road.

Sporting my new gear, I set off at 6am to Victoria Station to meet up with the team and take the train to Folkestone which was where we were to cross the Channel in the new Hovercraft (dinghies weren't the fashionable mode of transport then). There was a slight delay of over an hour because of a landslide at St Margarets. Finally aboard the new 'space age vessel', all were in good spirits and never mind it was still mid-morning, ordered our duty-free G&Ts. We set off but my G&T never touched my insides as the movement of the craft was so violent that my new suit got a thorough drenching. We soon realised that this mode of travel was going to be challenging.

Finally, arriving at Calais (before it was smartened up and then later filled with camps), we boarded a little sit up and beg puff puff train (not a TGV) and trundled across a bomb site area to find ahead of us, a square, drab, brick building with a large sign saying 'English Spoken'. Well, our fine dining consisted of chicken and chips, followed by the roughest crossing imaginable. It took four hours, as we had to go down the channel to try to find a safe and calmer place to cross. Everyone was vomiting. God, that was a fun day!

There was magic place called, 'A la Bonne Idée', in the midst of the forest of Compiègne. I remember it well, because once in our poverty-stricken days, I had stopped there to enquire about an overnight room and left in embarrassed haste when I had seen their prices. Years later, accompanied by a somewhat wealthier partner, we went to visit and to dine and stay there. It was a charming place with a very elegant restaurant full of Parisians and full silver service. We browsed the wine list and having suggested we come here, I was embarrassed by the prices – 200 euros per bottle was the norm. I suggested a mid-range Rhone wine. We laughingly said it was probably a bin end. The sommelier showed it to us with all the best sommelier decorum and poured us a small quantity each. My companion soon asked me to pass the wine to fill his glass. The minute my hand went out to touch the bottle, the sommelier was there to retrieve the bottle and then most definitely and somewhat defiantly placed it out of reach, having served another meagre measure. It was apparently infra dig for a lady to pour the wine! I bet that has changed.

Several years later, during the winter months, we

were invited by some friends we knew in the village to join them at a chateau in Champagne for an elaborate lunch, which had a champagne tasting with every course. It was a very plush and very expensive trip and we agreed to accompany them. At the last minute they asked if we would mind if another couple joined us. I was aghast. I knew the woman. She was the chav to outdo any chavs. However, we felt we had no choice but to go through with it.

We had the fine luncheon in the caves of the chateau, sharing a large oval table with two other international couples who spoke English. She, that woman, behaved as embarrassingly loudly and inappropriately as possible, so when the other couple invited us to dine at their hotel Champagne Royale that evening, I tried every which way to get out of it. No, they would send taxis for us.

It was the works, silver tureens all carried shoulder high by teams of waiters entering on cue, and on cue lifting the great lids with a polished flourish. This all really got rather messed up for them, by a certain person getting totally out of sync on all courses, and making totally inappropriate conversation about should she 'ave a baby or not?', as she passed forkfuls of food across the front of me for her fella to try. I don't remember what I ate. I know I had dreadful indigestion that night and hardly slept and escaped early, and gave them a wide berth for a long time.

However, once in a while it is lovely fine dining in a wonderful ambience with great service and delicacies you would not otherwise experience. Lovely

Raymond Blanc has certainly given us that here at Le Manoir aux Quat' Saisons. I do love the homage the French give to cuisine. Take this little paper place-mat, containing many famous writers views on food (*see photograph overleaf*). I came across it in a little bistro en route from Bordeaux to the Gers region. There we had the best steak and a really good wine. And I asked the proprietor if I might take a couple home with me, and I have them framed on my kitchen wall alongside an 'objet' given to me by a friend which is, I think, the key chest of a sommelier from the Burgundy region from whence comes my favourite Beaune wine.

An occasion that always stays with me, was when we were out scouring the reclaim yards for building materials, our project manager (yes, the one who eventually bunked off) pulled in for lunch at a Relais Routiers much favoured by lorry drivers and tradesmen, so you know they are good. We entered a large, functional refectory type room, where there were about forty-plus workmen seated on benches at trestle tables. I think, apart from the waitress, I was the only woman there and was served with the same entrée and plat du jour as everyone else. There were bottles of local wine on the table. The food was good, manners very civil and I never was made to feel out of place or uncomfortable there.

However, there is often the greatest joy to be had from sitting under a dappled sunlit table on a terrace, with good friends, with a plate of best Provençal tomatoes, sliced and interspersed with mozzarella cheese, drizzled with sea salt, pepper, garlic, olive oil, balsamic vinegar and crushed basil, and a crusty baguette, a glass of salmon pink Provençal Rosé, followed by sea bass and finished with Tarte Tatin and maybe a cheese board. Not much more has life to offer!

'Appetite increases with eating – thirst disappears with drinking.' (not sure about that one!).

FRANCOIS RABELAIS

'The Creator, in making it necessary for man to eat in order to live, invites him to it, through appetite and pleasure.' JEAN ANTHELME BRILLAT-SAVARIN

'The glutton begins to eat when he is no longer hungry.' ALPHONSE DAUDET

'If you are not capable of a bit of magic, then it is not worth you getting yourself mixed up in the kitchen.' COLETTE

'To eat well is to be in heaven.' PROVERBE CHINOISE

Epilogue

I will brush over the details of separation and losing my French house, mostly my fault, because they would I feel rather tarnish my tale. However, there is one last and rather dubious adventure, which I have pondered over sharing with you, because I would hate to leave you all with a sour taste in your mouth (about me, I mean) but in all honesty I am going to tell you of the worst thing I ever did and crave your understanding. My predicament was that I knew the locks to houses, here and in France had been changed so that I had no access to anything during the two-year financial wrangling. It was within two weeks of my having to sign away all rights to my little house in LGF and I had still been refused access to pick my stuff and collect a few of the many items I had picked up from *brocantes* over the years – another one of my passions – my soupières, a few paintings and pieces of Provençal porcelain and my books and clothes.

So with the incredible help and support of a couple of my dear friends, who live down there, I arranged to fly to Nice where they met me and then drove me to the village. Under cover of dark, I ascertained that the key to the big iron gates worked and we could get on to the terrace. The plan was that next morning, we would go via the terrace where there was one window that could be accessed, and we would break in. We arrived really early, and Phil insisted that we went to the gendarmerie and tell the police what we intended to do. They seemed perfectly sympathetic to the plight of a damsel who had been locked out of her home and immediately told us to *'Allez!'* Which we did.

The procedure involved carefully prizing a couple of slats out of the shutter, to give access to the pane of glass nearest the espagnolette (handle) to open the window. Phil wrapped a large cloth round his hand and smashed the glass with a piece of rock. He turned the handle and after carefully removing the shards of glass, we climbed in. Needless to say, not by nature being a thief, burglar or a miscreant, it felt a dreadful thing to be doing. We did our swift sweep of the house, passing items out to Roz, who stored them in the truck. Just as we were done, and I was at the lower level I tried the back door, which I had half-heartedly tried, expecting that lock to have been changed too. On trying again from the inside, to my horror the key turned! (All that had been needed was a bit of WD40.) That lock had not been changed and we needed never to have broken in! We retreated, clearing the mess, patching the window with some ply and restoring the slats with glue and beat it. They, my dear friends, stored my stuff until their next trip to England and dropped it all off to me then.

We immediately got in touch with a guy who was to repair the glass. He never went. I rang him over and over but he never went and I lost countless nights sleep worrying the mistral might blow the shutter in or that someone would break in. And all the time the final court hearing was looming and by then I had no money even to employ a solicitor let alone a barrister. So I wrote my own plea to the judge and attended the hearing with trepidation, but apart from the lady judge giving me a verbal slap on the wrist for not following procedure, I was allowed to keep what I had and no financial sanctions were issued against me or penalty for the escapade.

And so, dear reader, I come to the end of a lifetime of experiences in my beloved second home. I feel deeply honoured that I knew France after the war and the dark days of Vichy, and the beginning of the Marshall reconstruction, when it was still a deeply rural country, utterly beautiful, from mountains, forests, coastlines, and people who had an enormous pride in their culture, their *terroir*, wine, food and art. From the beauty of Paris with its magnetic pull on artists and writers, to the wondrous vineyards of Burgundy, down the Rhône/Saône Valley – to the little guys still sporting berets and strings of garlic, and the quiet back D roads where pootling along in a 2CV was just the job.

For me, sadly, I am told the end is near, and top of my bucket list is a few more days in my beloved France, speaking the language I have so loved and wrestled with all my life, drinking *un café* in a bistro or sipping a pastis, watching the world in a slow motion kind of way, giving time to the things that are important. So, I hold these memories fast in my heart and carry them with me on my way.

ACKNOWLEDGEMENTS

Lesley thanks…

her friend and designer Bridget Morley for her invaluable help, and a special thanks to Mungo Powney for his kind permission to use his painting 'milk crisis' as the stunning cover image.

her son Ciaran for being her mentor and unfailing sounding board and stimulating many memories, some of them shared.

her husband number 1 and 4, Douggie for hanging in there.

all the many friends who have been so supportive and encouraging.

Lesley Goldie née Herbert was born in 1943 and grew up in Romford, and Bromley, which put a bit of polish on her.

One of 5% of girls to go to university in 1961, she graduated with English Honours from Queen Mary, London, with a passion for acting.

Married four times, twice to the same man with whom she still lives, she has two sons, a stepdaughter, and countless step grandchildren. She has lived on the Norfolk/Suffolk border around Bungay for over fifty years, spending much of her time in the Charente and Provence. This has been her first venture into writing.

Printed in Great Britain
by Amazon